instant manager

taking control of work and life

inspiring leaders

balanced
SCORECARD

PROF MIKE BOURNE & PIPPA BOURNE

Hodder Arnold

A MEMBER OF THE HODDER HEADLINE GROUP

The publisher has used its best endeavours to ensure that the URLs for external websites referred to in this book are correct and active at the time of going to press. However, the publisher and the author have no responsibility for the websites and can make no guarantee that a site will remain live or that the content will remain relevant, decent or appropriate.

Orders: Please contact Bookpoint Ltd, 130 Milton Park, Abingdon, Oxon OX14 4SB. Telephone: (44) 01235 827720, Fax: (44) 01235 400454. Lines are open from 9.00 to 5.00, Monday to Saturday, with a 24-hour message answering service. You can also order through our website www.hoddereducation.co.uk.

British Library Cataloguing in Publication Data
A catalogue record for this title is available from the British Library.

ISBN-13: 978 0340 946497

First published in UK 2007 by Hodder Education, 338 Euston Road, London NW1 3BH in association with the Chartered Management Institute.

Typeset by Transet Limited, Coventry, England.
Printed in Great Britain for Hodder Education, a division of Hodder Headline, an Hachette Livre UK Company, 338 Euston Road, London NW1 3BH by Cox & Wyman Ltd, Reading, Berkshire.

Hodder Headline's policy is to use papers that are natural, renewable and recyclable products and made from wood grown in sustainable forests. The logging and manufacturing processes are expected to conform to the environmental regulations of the country of origin.

Impression number   10 9 8 7 6 5 4 3 2 1
Year   2012 2011 2010 2009 2008 2007

The Chartered Management Institute

The Chartered Management Institute is the only chartered professional body that is dedicated to management and leadership. We are committed to raising the performance of business by championing management.

We represent 71,000 individual managers and have 450 corporate members. Within the Institute there are also a number of distinct specialisms, including the Institute of Management Consultancy and Women in Management Network.

We exist to help managers tackle the management challenges they face on a daily basis by raising the standard of management in the UK. We are here to help individuals become better managers and companies develop better managers.

We do this through a wide range of products and services, from practical management checklists to tailored training and qualifications. We produce research on the latest 'hot' management issues, provide a vast array of useful information through our online management information centre, as well as offering consultancy services and career information.

You can access these resources 'off the shelf' or we can provide solutions just for you. Our range of products and services are designed to ensure companies and managers develop their potential and excel. Whether you are at the start of your career or a proven performer in the boardroom, we have something for you.

We engage policy makers and opinion formers and, as the leading authority on management, we're regularly consulted on a range of management issues. Through our in-depth research and regular policy surveys of members, we have a deep understanding of the latest management trends.

For more information visit our website **www.managers.org.uk** or call us on **01536 207307**.

Chartered Manager

Transform the way you work

The Chartered Management Institute's Chartered Manager award is the ultimate accolade for practising professional managers. Designed to transform the way you think about your work and how you add value to your organisation, as it is based on demonstrating measurable impact.

This unique award proves your ability to make a real difference in the workplace.

Chartered Manager focuses on the six vital business skills of:

- Leading people
- Managing change
- Meeting customer needs
- Managing information and knowledge
- Managing activities and resources
- Managing yourself

Transform your organisation

There is a clear and well-established link between good management and improved organisational performance. Recognising this, the Chartered Manager scheme requires individuals to demonstrate how they are applying their leadership and change management skills to make significant impact within their organisation.

Transform your career

Whatever career stage a manager is at Chartered Manager will set them apart. Chartered Manager has proven to be a stimulus to career progression, either via recognition by their current employer or through the motivation to move on to more challenging roles with new employers.

But don't take just our word for it...

Chartered Manager has transformed the careers and organisations of managers in all sectors.

- *'Being a Chartered Manager was one of the main contributing factors which led to my recent promotion.'*
Lloyd Ross, Programme Delivery Manager, British Nuclear Fuels

- *'I am quite sure that a part of the reason for my success in achieving my appointment was due to my Chartered Manager award which provided excellent, independent evidence that I was a high quality manager.'*
  Donaree Marshall, Head of Programme Management Office, Water Service, Belfast.

- *'The whole process has been very positive, giving me confidence in my strengths as a manager but also helping me to identify the areas of my skills that I want to develop. I am delighted and proud to have the accolade of Chartered Manager.'*
  Allen Hudson, School Support Services Manager, Dudley Metropolitan County Council

- *'As we are in a time of profound change, I believe that I have, as a result of my change management skills been able to provide leadership to my staff. Indeed, I took over three teams and carefully built an integrated team, which is beginning to perform really well. I believe that the process I went through to gain Chartered Manager status assisted me in achieving this and consequently was of considerable benefit to my organisation.'*
  George Smart, SPO and D/Head of Resettlement, HM Prison Swaleside

To find out more or to request further information please visit our website **www.managers.org.uk/cmgr** or call us on **01536 207429**.

Contents

CHAPTER 03

CHAPTER 04

CHAPTER 05

CHAPTER 08

CHAPTER 09

CHAPTER 10

Preface

The Balanced Scorecard has increased in popularity over the last 15 years. It started as a simple framework designed to help companies to structure their performance measures, but it has been developed into a much more encompassing strategy management tool. Great claims have been made, both for the widespread use of the Balanced Scorecard and for its efficacy, but there are critics. It is certainly not as widely used as some would suggest and there are occasions when Implementation fails or does not live up to initial expectations. However, there are many examples of organisations of all types who are putting it to excellent use.

In this book we take a pragmatic approach to the Balanced Scorecard and performance measurement and management in general. We will draw on well over a decade's experience of designing, implementing, using and refreshing measurement systems to explain what a Balanced Scorecard is and how it could work for you. We will take you through a process for designing a Balanced Scorecard, explaining how it can be implemented and the pitfalls to be avoided. In particular, we will illustrate how the scorecard can be used as a performance measurement and management tool throughout your organisation and how it can enhance performance.

Many organisations use the Balanced Scorecard to improve performance. But as a good friend once said:

> *'There are only three ways of improving performance. Firstly, you can actually improve performance. Secondly, you can cheat the system so that it appears performance is improved. Finally, you can simply lie about the performance achieved.'*

Improving performance is much harder to do than taking the other two options. We have all read the stories in the press of how public sector bodies have manipulated their performance to achieve government targets. We have heard the accounts of oil companies getting into difficulty over the way they report their oil reserves. You need to be aware of the unintended consequences of performance measurement, but if used in the right way it can be a powerful tool.

How to use this book
The chapters follow a logical sequence. We set out the context of performance measurement and the Balanced Scorecard and then trace the steps you would take to implement the scorecard in your organisation. The first five chapters cover how you decide what are the most important measures and then how to design those measures; how you embed your scorecard into the organisation and gain commitment from your people. The next three chapters deal with how you can use the Balanced Scorecard to manage your organisation, enabling it to become far more than a simple means of measuring what you are doing. You can use it to test out your business strategy, to turn that strategy into action and to ensure you are channelling everyone's energy in the same direction. We also take a look at how you can apply the Balanced Scorecard in various settings – different organisational structures, not-for-profit, public sector as well as commercial businesses. We end with an overview of alternatives to the Balanced Scorecard

and some tips on how you bring your performance measurement process together and prevent it from becoming 'just another initiative'. The chapters are self-contained but we would recommend that you read through them in order.

Pippa and Michael Bourne

Acknowledgements
We would like to thank all our friends in the Centre for Business Performance at Cranfield School of Management for their contribution to this book; Charles Carter and Julie Trim at the Institute of Chartered Accountants in England and Wales for their help and support; The Engineering and Physical Science Research Council for a series of research grants (GR/K53086, GR/L18655, GR/R56136/01 and Cranfield University's IMRC grant number 29).

01

What is a Balanced Scorecard?

Like all good tools, the Balanced Scorecard has evolved over time. From its origins in the late 1980s, successive development and improvements have occurred as users have learnt from practice. The simplest way of explaining what it is, is to start from its beginnings and show how it has developed.

The Balanced Scorecard originated in the United States in a company called Analogue Devices. Their scorecard had four measurement perspectives: financial, customer, process and people. Since 1992, Robert Kaplan and David Norton have been developing the Balanced Scorecard (see Figure 1.1). Their representation in the 1992 *Harvard Business Review* paper described the perspectives in terms of four questions:

- How do we look to our owners?
- How do we look to our customers?
- What must we excel at?
- How do we innovate and learn?

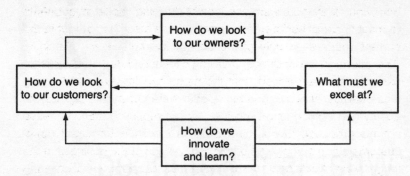

Figure 1.1: The questions that created the early Balanced Scorecard (adapted from Kaplan and Norton, 1992)

In essence, the Balanced Scorecard is about measuring the activities, processes and outputs that are most important for the success of the organisation. If these are truly the most important factors for success, they will naturally fall across the spectrum of activity within the organisation. It is difficult to think about even a simple organisation where being effective in only one field such as 'customer service' or 'new product development' (to pick two at random) will guarantee the long-term success of that enterprise. The processes and activities within an organisation are like a chain – they interlink and are only as strong as the weakest link. Excellence in one area (e.g. sales) can cause major problems in another (e.g. manufacturing). So, the balance of measures is equally as important as the individual measures themselves.

Why was the Balanced Scorecard developed?

One of the key motivations behind developing the Balanced Scorecard in the late 1980s and early 1990s was to reduce the focus placed on financial measures. They were seen as undermining competitiveness as they encouraged short-term behaviour. Managers were accused of delaying capital investments to meet financial performance targets, since these had a cost in the current year, whilst only giving benefit in future years. Similarly, discretionary expenditure was also manipulated. Advertising campaigns were delayed until the next financial year and training was often cancelled altogether. Costs were cut at the expense of quality and service levels reduced by not replacing staff. All these actions produced favourable results in the short term, but upset customers and damaged the competitiveness of the business in the longer term. Traditional performance measurement was beginning to be seen as backward looking, internally focused and future free. The Balanced Scorecard provided a solution by having four perspectives that created a balance across the organisation and afforded a view of what the future might bring.

How was balance achieved?

Financial stakeholders were still important in the Balanced Scorecard, but their wants and needs were balanced against the wants and needs of the customer. In this way, financial manipulations that improved financial returns, at the expense of the customer would rapidly become apparent and would be prevented.

But how can companies make money whilst still keeping their customers happy? The answer is in the alignment of the internal processes with the customers' requirements. By focusing on the key attributes their customers valued and designing processes that delivered these attributes, companies found they could deliver both to their customers and their financial stakeholders at the same time. This alignment was at the core of the original scorecard and is still one of the key features.

Being successful in beating the competition is not enough. Competitors are continuously improving their products and services and customers are becoming more demanding. To stay competitive, companies have to develop all the time. They have to develop new products, new services, new markets, new ways of doing things. They have to deal with new legislation, new trends in demand, new threats and opportunities in the business environment. To meet these changes they have to be 'fleet of foot', aware of what is happening around them and develop new skills to compete. This is where the innovation and learning perspective becomes important.

As you will see from Figure 1.2 opposite, the Balanced Scorecard balances:

- the internal with the external
- the financial with the non financial
- the past with the future

Financial performance is the consequence of all the other activities inside the business. It is an outcome and, as such, should not be manipulated directly. Improved financial performance, for a commercial concern, comes from having products and services that customers want and that are delivered to them effectively. Satisfied customers will then pay a realistic price for their purchases and buy again, leading to improved financial performance. Improvements in the lower-level perspectives of the scorecard, such as on-time delivery, should be leading indicators of improving performance of the higher-level perspectives such as financial performance.

What type of organisation can use the Balanced Scorecard?

As the scorecard is essentially a framework into which a set of measures is fitted, it can be used by any business or service provider. It is used by the public sector, 'not-for-profit' and commercial organisations of all sizes. It has also been adapted for individual use such as career or personal development. It can be

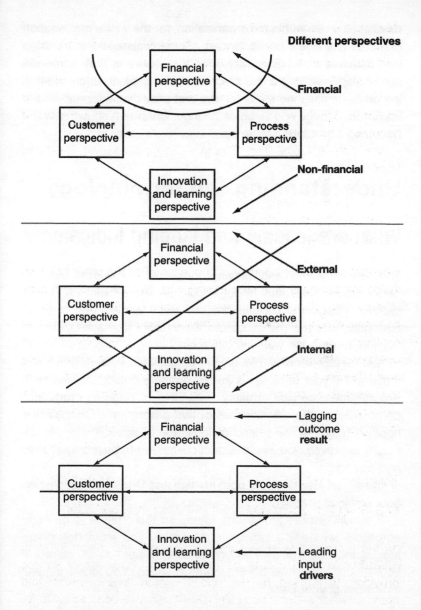

Figure 1.2: Different perspectives of the Balanced Scorecard

used at all levels within the organisation, for the whole organisation or just to examine a particular part. (Some organisations are using it to measure their HR activity or as a measure of their corporate social responsibility.) It is a mechanism for thinking about what is important, measuring those factors and providing information and insight to manage and instigate change. Chapter 8 shows how the Balanced Scorecard can be used in different settings.

Understanding the terminology

What are leading and lagging indicators?

The term 'leading and lagging indicators' is widely used in performance measurement but should be approached with some caution. Firstly, most indicators are both leading and lagging. Secondly, it is not the indicators themselves that are leading or lagging, but it is the way you use them.

Let us take an example. Is service quality a leading or lagging indicator? If your business is implementing a quality improvement programme, service quality will be a lagging indicator demonstrating the effectiveness of that programme. On the other hand, it may well be a leading indicator of sales. If the service quality improves, you would expect customers to be more satisfied and buy again.

Nearly all measures are both leading and lagging depending on how you look at them.

You will want to look to the future, so there tends to be more emphasis on leading indicators. However, you must not ignore lagging indicators as they tell you whether or not you are correct in your theory about how the organisation works. You ignore lagging indicators at your peril!

What are Strategy Maps?

Over the years, the Balanced Scorecard has evolved from the simple four-box model illustrated in Figure 1.1 to something altogether more useful. It was built on two concepts: firstly on the idea of leading and lagging indicators described above and secondly on the concept of mental models described below.

Eccles and Pyburn described in their paper of 1992 how senior managers could explain and share their views by the use of mental models. These are very simple devices that link together the objectives and assumptions about the business. Here is an example to illustrate this concept.

> **Mental model** The senior management team of an airline might believe that departure on time is important to customers. They expect that prompt departure will mean fewer delays across the network. It will also lead to arrivals being on time and these two benefits would increase customer satisfaction. Higher satisfaction will lead to customers being more willing to recommend the airline to friends and this would lead to a growth in sales. Figure 1.3 illustrates how this can be represented in a mental model.

This approach is very useful, as the model makes explicit the links between the various actions and outcomes. By drawing the model together as a team they create a shared set of assumptions about the drivers of performance.

The models were then incorporated into the four perspectives of the Balanced Scorecard and called 'Strategy Maps'. Figure 1.4 shows an example of this.

A better term for this might be 'success map' as the map highlights what you need to do to be successful. Robert Kaplan and David Norton put much emphasis on making 'strategy part of

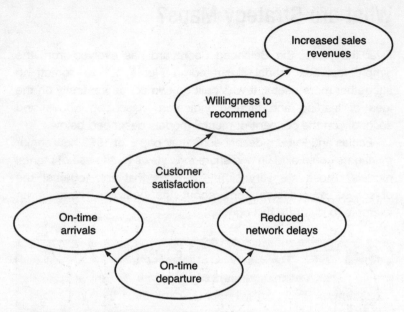

Figure 1.3: An example of a mental model

everyone's every day job'. But for many people, strategy is something someone else does. If you ask a group of people if they want to be successful, the resounding answer is 'Yes'. So success map is an easily understood term to which everyone can relate.

What are the steps involved on implementing a Balanced Scorecard?

The Balanced Scorecard is one tool used within a performance management process. There are steps which precede it, and steps to be taken following it. Figure 1.5 shows a generic approach, which suits most organisations. Here we will present the questions you should ask during each step of the process.

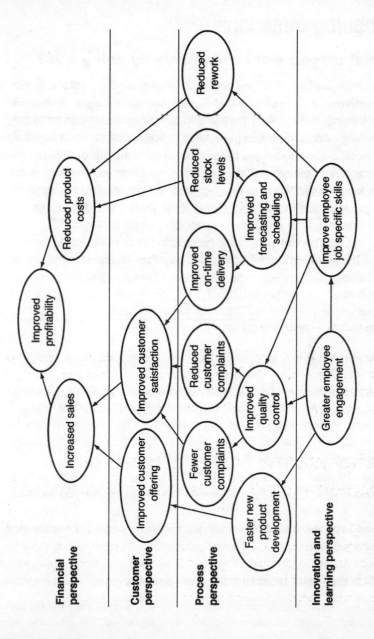

Figure 1.4: An example of a strategy map

Opening questions

What do you want to achieve by doing this?

The introduction of a performance management system is not something to be done without very careful thought. It is time consuming, it can cause feathers to be ruffled and it can have far-reaching effects on the organisation – both positive and negative. (Chapter 5 covers in more detail how to get the right conditions for successful implementation.) If there is no clear set of reasons for spending a significant amount of time on developing the system, or, indeed, commitment to doing it, at least from the top of the organisation, then you should probably not do it.

The first part of Chapter 2 highlights the benefits to be gained from using the Balanced Scorecard process. These benefits are far wider than simply recording progress. However, there are serious dangers in not doing it effectively. You can move your organisation in the wrong direction by spending time and resources on activities that do not matter and by alienating your employees.

Which part of the organisation do you choose?

The Balanced Scorecard is ideally designed to be applied in a self-contained business unit that has customers and suppliers and the goal of making a profit. But the scorecard can be applied at any level, so a choice has to be made. Do you approach the whole organisation, or conduct a pilot project in the business unit you think will most likely succeed with this approach? Do you content yourself with creating a unit level scorecard, or do you want to cascade the scorecard right down the organisation? Chapter 8 looks at a number of these issues and how you might apply the Balanced Scorecard in different settings.

Who do you involve in the project?

This will depend to some extent on why you are embarking on the process – and, of course, different people will be involved at

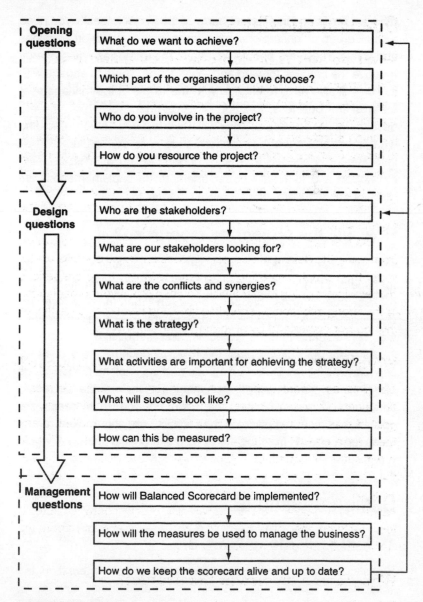

Figure 1.5: Steps for developing a Balanced Scorecard

different times and in different parts of the project. Ideally you need a small group of 'champions' who come from a variety oft functions and levels. These are people who have the enthusiasm and energy to move the process forward and to influence others to engage with it. You will also have to engage with the whole of the management team of the business, function or department for which you are developing the scorecard. They will need to be involved in deciding what is important and how performance is to be measured. Their involvement is needed to ensure understanding of what is being developed and to create commitment to its implementation. We discuss this requirement in detail in Chapter 5.

How will the project be resourced?

You will need a project management team as well as the senior managers. Initially, this may just be a project co-ordinator who makes sure things happen between the main scorecard development meetings. This resource is vital to ensure that actions stay on track and that the project is taken seriously.

As the project progresses, the role will become more onerous, especially as the measures are agreed and the implementation needs planning, co-ordinating and managing. Rolling out the scorecard takes effort in communicating the vision, chasing up the measures, collating the data and planning the reviews. You should be aware of these requirements from the start and make outline plans.

Design questions

Who are the stakeholders?

Stakeholders are people who have a significant interest in the organisation. They could be: owners, shareholders, customers, suppliers, employees and even regulators. You should start by understanding what the key stakeholders (as a minimum, the customers and owners) want from the business. When working with companies we usually ask the question 'which stakeholders' requirements do you need to consider when deliberating on the future of the business?'.

What are your stakeholders looking for?

You need to identify what the requirements are of your various stakeholders, both now and in the future. This should be done as clearly and precisely as possible. We will discuss this in detail in Chapter 3.

What are the conflicts and synergies?

The stakeholder groups can have very different perspectives on the organisation and some expectations can be diametrically opposed. In a service organisation, employees may want limited out-of-hours working, whereas customers may want 24-hour service. In a water company, the regulator may want to limit price increases, whereas shareholders will want an increase in return for their investment. The relationships are not always as simple as they look and are worth investigating in depth because what may seem initially to be a conflict might actually be a synergy.

What is the strategy?

Organisations may exist to satisfy their stakeholders, but there has to be a strategy for doing this that allows the organisation to survive and prosper. The strategy exists to set the direction that balances the stakeholders' and the organisation's needs. Leading from the strategy will be a set of plans and actions which can be measured. So, a clear strategy (or, perhaps understanding what the strategy means) is a prerequisite for putting in place a performance management system.

What activities are important for achieving the strategy?

Many activities may stem from the strategy and the plans underlying it, but are they all really necessary? Do they add value or are they in existence because they form part of they way things have always been done? How do the activities interlink? One way of simplifying what can be a complex area is to use a success map. This is described in detail in Chapter 3.

What will success look like?

How will you know you are performing these activities well and satisfying your stakeholders? This is about defining what success will look like when you achieve it. Having a clear picture of the desired result, communicates the direction in which you want to go, is motivating and provides the means to measure progress.

How will this be measured?

Ensuring measures are measuring what you intend may sound obvious but it is not as easy as it first appears. Also, the adage 'what gets measured gets done' holds true. By creating a set of measures you have indicated where effort is to be directed. If effort has been misdirected, resources will be squandered. The effects, if you get your measures wrong, can be quite considerable. Chapter 4 deals in detail with designing appropriate measures.

Management questions

How will the Balanced Scorecard be implemented?

Implementing the Balanced Scorecard In any organisation is a significant task. It will require careful planning, resources and significant persistent management effort. Chapter 5 will provide guidance about how to do this and examples of pitfalls to be avoided.

How will the measures be used to manage the business?

Having set up the Balanced Scorecard and designed the performance measures, you now need to devote time to using the information to best effect. In part, this links back to the first question: why are you embarking on this project? From your design work, you will know which areas of the business or process are most critical to success, which are the priorities and which are the 'quick wins' likely to influence some of the detractors to the project. This is the stage when you agree a routine for ensuring results from the measurements are being analysed and actions taken as a result. Chapter 6 examines how measures can be used and describes behaviours that differentiate between high and low performing organisations.

How do you keep the scorecard alive and up to date?

Performance measurement is not a 'one-off' project. The framework for the process may stay the same but the content will need to change in line with changes to the strategy and the environment in which the organisation operates. (Think about the rapid rise in importance of corporate responsibility for many businesses. Even five years ago, measuring, say, environmental sustainability of activity was not as high on the list of factors for success.) Failing to revise the measures regularly and check they are still pertinent will stifle development or bring the Balanced Scorecard into disrepute. Chapter 7 deals with this in some detail.

Conclusion

By now you should know what a Balanced Scorecard is and how it has evolved over time. You have an understanding of the terminology and of the process you need to undertake if you are going to implement a Balanced Scorecard. So there is one last question to answer before you embark on the project; 'Will it be worth the effort?' This is the question we address in Chapter 2, with the rest of the book being dedicated to the processes of design, implementation, use and review.

Good luck!

INSTANT TIP

You need multiple perspectives of performance to manage your business successfully.

02

What are the strengths and weaknesses of this approach to measuring performance?

Introduction

This chapter begins with a section on the purposes for which you can use the Balanced Scorecard, with practical examples of how it has been used or misused in particular circumstances. Although there are many good examples of how the Balanced Scorecard can be put to good effect, there are also many organisations which have wasted a great deal of time implementing it to no avail, so we also examine stages at which it can fail. We will finish the chapter by discussing the evidence around whether or not implementing a Balanced Scorecard makes a difference to business performance and identify situations where we do not think a Balanced Scorecard is appropriate.

How can you use the Balanced Scorecard?

A good measurement system will help to:

- establish your current position
- communicate direction
- align action to strategy
- stimulate action in the most important areas for your business
- facilitate learning
- influence behaviour

The process of arriving at a good measurement system will help you to think through your strategy, examine conflicts between the various stakeholders in your organisation and decide what actions are necessary to achieve your objectives.

Establishing the current position

It may seem obvious, but knowing where your starting point is may not be as simple as it sounds. Many organisations rely on anecdotal evidence to the extent it becomes ingrained as 'fact' when it is not. Statements like: 'We know we offer the fastest delivery times in our business'; 'Our customers are delighted with the service we offer'; 'Our employees love working here', may well have been true at one time but no longer stand up to close scrutiny when researched in more detail. Hard though the lesson can be, understanding the real position is vital in understanding what action is necessary and in avoiding complacency. Beliefs can be strong and it is through production of hard evidence that firmly held views can be changed.

A waste of money?   The most articulate and vocal customers in one 'not for profit' organisation maintained consistently that the newsletter sent to all customers was almost never read and was therefore a waste of time and money. A survey of all customers revealed, however, that two thirds of customers did read it and its withdrawal caused concern, even amongst the detractors.

Do you really know the answer?   When working in a board mill producing the cardboard liners for boxes, we regularly made two different weights of the same product: 200 gsm and 300 gsm (grams per square metre). The machine had originally been designed to produce the heavier weights, so produced the 300 gsm product much faster and more easily than the 200 gsm product. One day, returning from a visit with the mill manager, Glyn, we got into a heated argument about how much of the two products the company made and sold. Glyn was convinced that we made substantially more 200 gsm than 300 and was shocked when I proved otherwise with the figures. His perception had been based on the length of time and number of problems he had encountered in production, which distorted the true picture.

Establishing your position is important as a basis for:

- establishing progress between last year and this year
- comparing performance of similar departments or branches within the company
- benchmarking with competitors

Unless you measure accurately and consistently from a solid base line, the whole ethos of measurement will be undermined and results will be meaningless. You are also in danger of making the wrong decisions.

Communicating direction

The act of creating a set of measures immediately focuses attention on particular set of activities and outcomes. The measures set out what is essential for the success of the organisation and also, very importantly, what is not.

You get what you pay for!   Take the example of a training business. For several years one of the components used to calculate the bonus paid to business development managers was based on numbers of new customers introduced in that year. The number of new customers was a key performance indicator. However, it was becoming clear that the profitability of each new contract was steadily decreasing. Almost without realising it, the business had moved from one which offered high-quality management development at a realistic price to high profile companies, to one which offered a cut-price service which also meant cutting corners. This happened when business development managers, conscious of their targets, focused on attracting new customers at almost any price. Whilst there is nothing wrong with offering a less expensive service to a larger number of customers, the structure of the business was not set up to do that. Over time, the number of customers had increased but the high-profile customers had drifted away and the overall profitability of the business had dwindled. Including in the performance indicators a measure of price and profitability per contract and changing the means by which the business development managers' bonus was calculated helped to redress the balance. The direction for this business was re-stated as 'offering a high quality service to a smaller number of defined businesses' and the measurement system clearly reflected that.

Aligning action to strategy

'What gets measured gets done.' How many organisations spend time and money devising a strategy, which then remains sitting on the shelf, known only to the elite few at the top of the organisation? It is possible to see an organisation's stated strategy and then look at what is actually happening and see very little link between the two. The example above shows how, as well as communicating the direction of the business, crystallising the strategy into a set of measures can help to align action with the strategy. If employees' performance is to be judged against certain criteria, that is where most of them will concentrate their effort.

Performance measurement should make goals and objectives explicit and bring the strategy to life. If communicated in the right way, it should be possible to create a culture of achievement in which individuals no longer work in the dark but are clear about their roles and what their contribution is to be in creating a successful organisation. A good performance measurement system will act as a motivator, showing people what is expected of them and how they are progressing.

Are you aligning your measues with strategy?

In one small not-for-profit organisation the stated objectives for a particular team were to:

- build relationships with policy makers for lobbying purposes;
- increase the number of members (growth was a key aspect of the strategy);
- raise the profile of the organisation;
- improve media coverage of the organisation and its concerns.

However, the following activities and performance levels were measured:

- number of events run;
- number of members attending events (*not the number of new people who were not yet members*);
- number of meetings attended (*not the quality of putput from those meetings*);
- number of press releases sent out (*not those picked up by the quality press or journals where the articles might have made a difference to the organisation's causes*).

Clearly, the objectives and activities measured have some link but not necessarily a direct causal relationship. The result was that members of the small team were constantly attending meetings, sending out press releases and arranging events. These were marketed heavily to existing members of the organisation who were more likely to attend and therefore enabled the team to tick the box on target number of attendees. This was done instead of targeting new people who might be attracted to membership by attending the event, but who would be harder to reach. Part of the reason for setting up the measurements in this way was because the IT system made it difficult to differentiate between new people and existing members. Another reason was the difficulty they encountered in trying to measure profile.

Intangibles are difficult to measure but not impossible – through awareness surveys, for example. If measurement of a particular aspect proves too difficult or expensive to be worthwhile, it is sometimes better not to have a measure at all, rather than to include one which will result in actions which are not channelling energies into achieving the objectives of the strategy.

Stimulating action

Few organisations have unlimited resources, so all resources should be directed as efficiently as possible towards fulfilling the most important requirements of the business. The question is: 'Are there mechanisms in place to ensure that is happening?' Using the Balanced Scorecard can help in ensuring that physical resources as well as people's time are being used for the most appropriate purpose.

Choosing the measure to drive action   I installed a Balanced Scorecard in a small instrument company, which used that approach for over four years to run the business. During that time the measures were produced monthly and reviewed at the senior management meetings.

The company was highly customer focused, but we had great difficulty in making progress on the measure of customer complaints. The problem lay in trying to define a complaint. Was this just the formal letter received, or did it include comments made to the sales engineers over the telephone? There were very few formal letters, so the number of complaints received each month relied on the person who talked to the customer deciding to register the conversation as a complaint.

How did we deal with this? We decided to celebrate customer complaints, rather than focusing on eliminating them. The company realised that if we targeted a reduction in complaints, we would simply stop them being recorded and all the useful information received through the complaints process would be lost. At each monthly meeting, the quality manager reported the complaints together with his analysis of the cause, and we prioritised actions as a result.

If customer complaints were not going to be the key measure of product quality, what else could be used? The measure finally agreed was 'customer returns', chosen because it was more objective. The customer had decided to return the product, either because it did not work, because there was a performance problem or because it did not meet his or her requirements. These were all serious issues, and, as returned products were immediately booked into the computer system, we believed this measure was robust. Reducing the number of customer returns was something the company could target.

In fact the number of customer returns had been an issue for several years and the quality manager had been frustrated because his reports had been ignored. This all changed when we started to plot the graph of customer returns. The quality manager also plotted the number of despatches on the same graph and there was an immediate recognition that the company had a significant problem. As the volumes of despatches increased, the number of returns increased at a disproportionately high rate. In other words, returns were increasing dramatically at busy times. The end result was that resources were dedicated to solving this serious problem.

Some measures can stimulate rapid and focused action. From the example above, the 'customer returns' measure was a good example as the measure raised an issue that could be simply diagnosed and acted upon. Other measures such as 'turnover per employee' or 'return on capital employed' are also important measures as they monitor the real financial health of the organisation. But they are much harder to influence as they are an outcome of the activity of the whole company. These measures should stimulate action, but can be seen as too hard to tackle as causes are complex.

Facilitating learning

There are two aspects to this: firstly using the learning perspective of the Balanced Scorecard to ensure the organisation is not remaining static but taking an innovative approach to its business; and, secondly, the learning that comes from reflecting on what the outcomes of the measures mean. Using a good set of measures to provoke debate about the key issues of the business strategy should provide information for making better decisions. Two important questions are:

● Do the measures show how well you are implementing the strategy?
● Do the measures show that the strategy is broadly correct in enabling you to fulfil the organisation's objectives?

At an operational level, using the analysis of measures over time will help you to understand better the dynamics of your business and identify trends at an early stage so action can be taken.

The Martin's Motor Group The Martin's Motor Group, a long-established family business, was concerned their revenue from their service department was falling, despite performing well against most of the measures on their Balanced Scorecard. They believed they were offering a good personal service and frequently received complimentary comments from their customers. They knew their charges were at least in line with their competitors' and were fairly certain that in some cases they charged less. Nevertheless, they were losing customers.
They believed their customers wanted:

- work to be completed to the required standard by a specified time
- their car to be cleaned before return
- work to be carried out within agreed price limits – or agreement sought for extra work discovered during the service
- invoices and service reports to be available on collection of the car
- their car to be parked on the forecourt for speedy exit

Further research revealed their customers did, indeed, want all the above, but even more than that, they wanted:

- a courtesy car to be available when necessary.
- collection and delivery of their vehicle.
- longer opening hours at the end of the day and on Saturday afternoons.

Over the years, more of their customers were working and finding it difficult to take their cars in for servicing during working hours. The garage in the next town was aware of this and offered a collection and delivery service and longer opening hours. Although they were slightly more expensive than Martin's, customers found this service far more convenient. Martin's had offered a good service in the past and continued to do so for a dwindling number, but they had failed to take account of the changing circumstances of the majority of their customers.

Smiling The management of a convenience store group in North America was concerned about the competition from big supermarket chains. A strategy was developed to protect the company's competitive position, based on engaging with the customer. So staff were trained to greet customers, smile and converse with them as they shopped or checked out.

Keen to know what impact the training had made, it was decided to audit the implementation of the project. Mystery shoppers were hired to assess the behaviour of staff in each store. Did they smile?

The results were mixed, but the evaluation team found that many of the busy stores were not 'smiling'. This prompted a further analysis, which showed that the stores with the highest 'smile' rating were not the best performers.

What was happening? What the management team learnt was that 'smiling' was not always appropriate. Convenience stores are busy in the rush hour, before and after work. This is also true at lunchtime. When the store is busy, customers don't want to be greeted, they want to be served quickly. So in those periods, smiling was not appropriate. However, at quieter times, engaging with the customer and smiling was effective, so the employees had to learn to adapt their behaviour.

Influencing behaviour

The Balanced Scorecard should enable you to encourage the right behaviour and discourage inappropriate actions. In the example of the training company at the beginning of this chapter ('You get what you pay for'), business development managers were discouraged from attracting too many low price contracts by a change in the way their performance was measured and rewarded. Defining the measures carefully should influence people's behaviour to achieve the goals you have set for the organisation. It should also enable you to motivate people and create a sense of purpose by showing the progress that is being made towards achieving these goals.

Playing to strengths The course-running department of a university was staffed by highly capable people, who had originally been recruited for their excellent interpersonal skills. The 'courses' they ran were essentially PR events. As time went by, it became imperative for the university to increase its income. Turning the course operation into a commercial venture was seen as a good way of doing that. However, in the early stages it was a failure. Some of the team left, courses ran at a loss and morale was very low.

The project to turn the department into a money-making operation was reviewed and several new elements introduced, not least of which was a major communications exercise. The Balanced Scorecard was also used, involving the team in its development. One of the key measurements devised by the team was the increase in the number of season ticket holders. This measure used to good effect with the team members' strength in building up relationships with their customers (something they all enjoyed) and generated regular income. The results of this measure were displayed colourfully in a prominent position in the office. Over a very short period the number of season ticket holders increased substantially but, even more importantly, the team members began to realise that building good relationships with customers was not at odds with making sales.

In summary, then, the Balanced Scorecard can be used for:

- deciding what the key drivers of performance are
- refocusing and simulating activity on these key business drivers
- drawing attention to goals and targets
- creating a culture of achievement
- identifying in advance any trends affecting the organisation so that changes can be made in advance.

Load, aim fire If you are trying to shoot something it is important that you first load your rifle, you then take careful aim and finally you fire! Not surprisingly if you miss out any if these steps you will not get the result you are looking for.

The same is true of performance measurement. Here the mantra is:

'Data, Insight, Action'

- If you have the wrong data, then you will make the wrong inferences and take the wrong actions.
- If you have the right data but draw the wrong insights, then again you will take the wrong actions.
- If you have the right data and generate the right insights but then either fail to take action or take the wrong action, you will fail.

So, like shooting with a rifle, there is a set of steps to get right and in the right order!

Where do Balanced Scorecards fail?

The section above demonstrates the benefits to be gained by using the Balanced Scorecard. However, there are a number of different stages at which Balanced Scorecards fail. Some of these are covered in Chapter 5 in more detail but it is worth noting an overview.

Failure to complete the design

If a good process is used, this is a very rare occurrence. Most teams can work through the process of designing the measurement system quite easily unless a sudden, major and unexpected event occurs.

Failure of implementation

This happens far more regularly. It is relatively simple to enable the management team to work together to develop a theoretical Balanced Scorecard with the set of measures. Implementing those measures, collecting the data, analysing it, producing the graphs and so on takes time and effort. It involves other people and this is the stage at which most Balanced Scorecard initiatives fail. A Balanced Scorecard is never fully implemented until the measures are displayed to the whole organisation. This may be simply putting the graphs up on display on the office walls, or on an intranet with open access. However, we believe that until they are available to the whole organisation, they are viewed merely as a management toy.

Failure of use

This tends to happen over time if managers are not consistently making use of the performance measures. Designing and implementing the scorecard is an expensive and time-consuming process, but that is only the start. Without review and visible action being taken, based on the results of the measures, commitment will be lost and the scorecard will decay.

Failure of revision

This can be extremely dangerous. Having a high-performing Balanced Scorecard that is out of date can take your organisation very efficiently in the wrong direction. When the environment changes, the strategy needs to be revised. One very effective way of communicating a new strategy is to realign the performance measures. Failure to do this will result in a strategy to do one thing and employees being guided to do another. In nearly all situations, the measures win! Chapter 7 reviews how we keep the scorecard up to date.

Failure of commitment

One of the overriding reasons for failure is lack of commitment. This can occur at any point: at the beginning when it can be seen as 'yet another initiative'; shortly after implementation if no quick results are seen; well into the process when it has not been kept up to date and people no longer see the value. Maintaining commitment is essential until the approach becomes a way of life for your organisation.

Does the Balanced Scorecard make a difference?

There are hosts of studies that attempt to answer this question (see Franco and Bourne (2004), which identified 100 studies). From an academic perspective it is very difficult to show that a tool, such as the Balanced Scorecard, actually makes a positive impact on the performance of the business.

We were extremely pleased to see the improvement in performance of the three companies we had worked with in the year following their successful implementation of the Balanced Scorecard. Unfortunately, we cannot take all the credit, as there was also a significant upturn in the market at the same time as the scorecards were being implemented. Removing these other effects from your analysis is not easy and to do this properly requires controlling for a wide range of variables that may have an impact on your research.

The academic evidence on whether the scorecard makes a difference is mixed because it is difficult to isolate cause and effect. In practice, however, many companies believe the Balanced Scorecard makes a positive impact on their businesses.

Interestingly, the companies we know have succeeded with their scorecards are those who believe it will make a big difference to their development. The senior management of these organisations see it is a new way of managing the business. In our experience, those who see the scorecard as 'being a better way of measuring' are less successful.

When should I not implement a Balanced Scorecard?

There are circumstances under which it is not advisable to implement a Balanced Scorecard. These are:

1. When the company is in a crisis.
2. When you are operating in a very turbulent environment.

Company in crisis

If the company is in crisis, you obviously need to take the initial steps required to save the business first before starting on a

Balanced Scorecard project. The tools we use here are useful for setting strategic direction, but the implementation takes too long to be useful in a crisis. Our advice is to settle the situation first, then use the scorecard at a later date to take you to the next stage of development.

After 9/11 After the attacks on the World Trade Centre in New York, all flights were grounded in the United States for several days. In fact, it took several months for people to get back to flying as usual. Even large companies found themselves in difficulties.

One airline had just implemented its Balanced Scorecard when it was hit by the aftermath of the 9/11 attacks on New York. The crisis caused the company to ditch the scorecard and focus on three key measures:

- passenger numbers
- fuel expenditure
- cash flow.

These were the three indicators the management had to watch. Fuel, because it was a big variable cost, passenger numbers to gauge the recovery and cash flow to survive. It was well over a year later that the company felt in a position to reintroduce its scorecard.

A very turbulent environment

If the environment is unstable and the business is changing exceptionally quickly, you should be aware that a formal Balanced Scorecard might mean that you react too slowly. In this environment it is important you use the latest information available.

Under such circumstances, using a few key performance indicators that change rapidly to reflect current management thinking will be a better approach.

Conclusion

In this chapter we have looked at what you can do with your Balanced Scorecard if you get it right. To get it right you need to:

- measure the right thing
- measure in the right way
- manage the right way.

In the next chapter, we will focus on helping you to decide what to measure by incorporating your business objectives in a success map. This is all about 'measuring the right thing'. In Chapter 4, we will describe a process to help you design your measures, so that 'you measure the right way'. Chapter 6 looks at how you manage with measures and provides a set of tools and approaches to help you 'manage the right way'.

INSTANT TIP

You have to believe in the Balanced Scorecard for it to work.

03

How do you decide what to measure?

Introduction

This chapter will show you three different approaches for setting objectives that are linked to your strategy and ultimately help you to decide what to measure. Firstly, we will describe the 'what? / how?' process used in developing a success map. Secondly, we will describe a customer and stakeholder process, which can be used to develop a better understanding of the requirements and pressures on your business. Finally, we will describe a multi-stakeholder success mapping process, which combines elements of the first two approaches. But before we describe each of the approaches, we will just explain what we mean by taking a process approach to developing the scorecard.

The process approach

All three approaches can be applied as processes. During a series of workshops, the facilitator will take the team through the exercises and discussion using the exercises and tools decsribed below. The idea of a process is that it structures the discussion so you are able to use the time efficiently.

What is the role of the facilitator?

The facilitator's role is primarily that of owning and running the process. He or she should:

- explain the process
- explain the tools being used
- ask the questions
- interpret the team's input
- clarify any misunderstandings
- complete the forms
- referee the debate
- draw the debate to a consensus and conclusion.

Ideally, the facilitator should be neutral and limit their participation to running the process. He or she should not make content inputs, although challenging the input made by the team is part of the role. You will have to consider whether you have an individual of sufficient stature and neutrality to undertake this role in your organisation or whether you need an external facilitator to help you.

Who should be involved in the team?

You should create a team specifically to develop the Balanced Scorecard. The team should include the senior managers who have responsibility for running the business. Typically, this will be the managing director or general manager and his or her direct reports as well as other knowledgeable individuals. We will return to the topic of participation in Chapter 5 when we discuss implementation. Just one word of warning: do not delegate this task to a 'staff' team. Senior line managers need to be involved and should make the time to create the Balanced Scorecard. If they do not, it is our experience that the project will fail.

What are the tools?

The tools include the success map, the customer/stakeholder objectives sheet and the performance measure record sheet (covered in more detail in Chapter 4).

These are the forms, which help the facilitator to ask questions and structure answers in a way that adds value to the debate. They capture important elements of the discussion as it develops and form a record of how the team's thinking has evolved. We will describe how they are used throughout the next three sections of this chapter.

We will now look at the three approaches, which will help you to decide what to measure.

The 'what? how?' approach

Firstly, we will explain how you use this approach in practice. Secondly, we will give you an example of a success map created by using this approach. Thirdly, we will go on to outline why the approach is so powerful.

The 'what/how?' approach will help you to turn organisational goals into objectives and then to create a 'success map'. In essence, you follow a logical sequence of questions, asking what you need to achieve and how you will do it. The result will be a set of objectives essential to the success of the organisation. At a later workshop, you can translate these into specific performance measures (see Chapter 4), but the objective here is to create a success map. This is very similar to the approach adopted by Kaplan and Norton (1996) in their book, *Translating Strategy into Action*. Companies such as BT have used variations of this approach.

The role of the facilitator is to encourage debate around the core objective of the organisation. Once this has been established and agreed, the facilitator steers the discussion from 'what is to be achieved?' to 'how should this be achieved?'

For example, a company wishes to increase its financial returns. Having agreed the 'what', the debate moves on to 'how' this should be achieved. The management team may identify two main methods – growing sales revenues and reducing operating costs. After debating what is meant by these concepts, these two objectives now become the main 'hows' for implementing the strategy (see Figure 3.1).

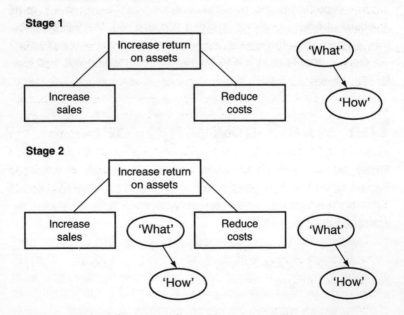

Figure 3.1: A 'what/how' example

The questioning should now turn to 'how the sales revenues will be increased?' and 'how the operating costs will be cut?' The 'hows' for increasing returns now become the 'whats' for the next level down in the success map.

The facilitator should ask:

- 'If what we are trying to achieve is increased sales revenue, how are we going to do this?'
- 'If what we are trying to achieve is reduced operating costs, how are we going to do this?'

This is then repeated at the next level, using the 'what? / how?' questioning to cascade the objectives.

With your first attempt, you will get a very complicated success map containing many suggestions and links. Do not be put off by the complicated nature of your first attempt, but it will need to be refined. Ideally, in the first workshop you should attempt to create an initial unedited draft of the success map. This can be tidied up into a presentation and distributed before the second workshop. This will give the team time to reflect on what has been produced. The second workshop should be used to review the success map, asking critical questions about what has been developed. You should aim to identify the key 'what/how' relationships, rather than capturing all the relationships that exist. You should also ask the 'why?' question. By asking 'why?' you can start at the bottom of the success map and test all the links to the top of the map. For example, you should ask:

'Why do we want employees to be satisfied?'
'Because we believe happy employees stay with the company longer.'

'Why do we want employees to stay with us longer?'
'Because we believe longer serving employees have better knowledge and skills.'

'Why do we want employees to have better knowledge and skills?'
'Because we believe these employees give better service
to the customer.'

'Why do we want better customer service?'
'Because we believe that better customer service leads to
greater customer retention.'

'Why do we want greater customer retention?'
'Because we believe greater customer retention increases
sales revenues.'

'Why do we want increased sales revenues?'
'Because we believe increased sales revenues result in
greater profitability, which is our main top level objective in
this success map.'

In this way, you can test the logic of the success map. For each objective in the success map, the subordinate objective should explain 'how' it is to be achieved. For each subordinate objective, the higher objective should explain 'why' it is to be undertaken. Ideally, by the end of the second workshop you should have a success map the management team can agree on. This can then be used as the basis for your scorecard.

An example of a success map

Figure 3.2 shows an example of a success map developed for a training business. Ideally, you will be able to get the final success map on a single page of A4. However, as you cascade the success map down your organisation, you will need to create other success maps that fit in with what you have developed, We will discuss this in more detail in Chapter 8.

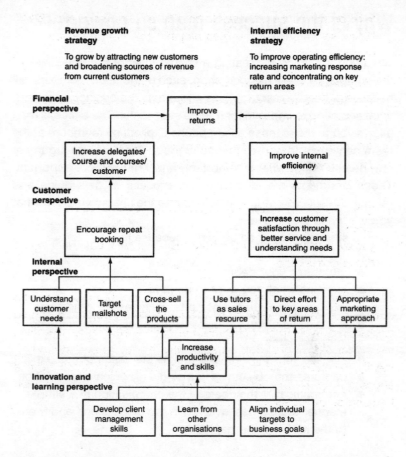

Figure 3.2: A version of the Balanced Scorecard developed for the Chartered Management Institute's training operation

Why is the success map so powerful?

What you are doing is creating a shared view of the objectives of the company. Before the workshop, each of the team members will have his or her own assumptions about how the business runs and what you need to improve for it to be successful. The success map allows you to make these assumptions explicit, so members of the team can share their own mental models. There will be argument and debate about what is important, and what is more important. These arguments are all part of the process of developing and refining the success map and help create the shared vision of what you are trying to achieve.

The success map is so powerful because it:

- structures your debate
- explains what you want to achieve
- explains how you are going to achieve your objectives
- explains why you are undertaking specific projects and improvements
- clarifies your thinking and makes the assumptions explicit
- captures the objectives in a single graphical presentation
- communicates the goals of the organisation in a simple manner to all those involved in the discussions and then to the rest of the organisation.

We know from our experience and from surveying companies that only some 5 per cent of organisations have success maps. However, we also know that companies who develop success maps greatly benefit from the process and find it a very useful communication tool for explaining the strategy to the rest of the business.

The customer and stakeholder process

This second approach is extremely useful for identifying what the business needs to achieve to satisfy the requirements of its customers and major stakeholders. The approach was developed at Cambridge University ('Getting the Measure of your Business', Neely et al, 1996) and uses customer and stakeholder needs as the basis for creating the top-level business objectives.

Ideally, you should do this in a facilitated workshop with the whole of the senior management team. In this approach, the team works through the following steps:

1. Identifies the needs of the customers.
2. Identifies the needs of the main stakeholders.
3. Consolidates these needs into a single coherent list.
4. Creates a success map from this list.

Firstly, customer needs are identified using the headings of quality, time, cost/price and flexibility. You should ask the team to articulate precisely what their customers are looking for, both now and in the future.

Secondly, stakeholder needs are identified. Stakeholders should be any group whose needs you want the organisation to take into account when creating the scorecard.

Thirdly, the two lists of objectives are blended into a single list, which meets the requirements of both the customer and the stakeholders.

Fourthly, you should use this list to create a success map.

Which tool should you use?

The tool for this approach is found in Figure 3.3. The tool splits the requirements of the customers from the requirements of the other stakeholders, so that each can be addressed in turn.

The prompts of 'quality, time, cost/price, flexibility and other' are to stimulate the team's input. It is not necessary to complete each box. The facilitator should start with identifying the customer requirements first, then those of the stakeholders, before attempting to create a combined list. The next few sections will take you through the detail of how this is done.

	Customer needs ➔	Objective ⬅	Stakeholder needs
Quality			
Time			
Cost/price			
Flexibility			
Other			

Figure 3.3: The Customer, Stakeholder Objectives Sheet (Adapted from Neely et al., 1996)

Who are your customers?

This is a seemingly easy question that bears more careful consideration. The customer may not actually be the consumer. Take the example of the purchase of a toy. If you own a toyshop, the customer is the parent and the consumer is the child. The child may be looking for fun, colour, softness and adorability. The parent may be thinking about health and safety, cost and noise level. But if you are the toy manufacturer, you will have a different perspective. Your customer will now be the toyshop and the chain is even longer.

So in developing your understanding of the customers' needs, it is important to consider the direct customer, as well as all those in the chain to the consumer. This is because:

- If you cannot persuade the shop to stock the product, it will not be there for the parent to buy.
- If the parent is worried about safety or disruptive noise, then there is an issue.
- If the child is present at the time of purchase, but not interested, again the sale may well not happen.

Understanding the customer and the consumer is not just the preserve of the business-to-consumer setting. In Figure 3.4 we show an example of the different needs in a business-to-business environment. Here we show the situation facing a brick manufacturer, who has architects to contend with as well.

When we are working with companies to understand their customer requirements, we deliberately start with the consumer, and then move step by step through the links in the chain to the businesses' immediate customers. In this example we asked the team to put themselves into the minds of the house owner, then the architect, then the builder and finally the builders' merchant. In this way we structure and focused the debate.

	House Owner	Architect	Builder	Builders' Merchant
Quality	Must last; Must look nice	Special effects for interesting designs; Must look nice	Easy to lay; Undamaged on arrival	Doesn't want returns
Cost	Some importance for overall price of house	Less important	Quite important	Interested in profit margin
Time	Important that house is completed on time	No particular concern	Must arrive when promised; Short lead time	Must arrive when promised; Short lead time
Flexibility	No particular interest	Wide product range from which to choose	No particular concern	Wide product range to attract wide range of customers

Figure 3.4: The differing needs of consumers and customers

Many businesses will have a variety of customer and product groups. The key here is to analyse the needs of each of those groups starting with the most important, which may not be the biggest. A higher percentage of your profit may come from a smaller group of customers who pay the most for your products or services.

How do you define your customers' needs?

Having established who your customers are and broadly what they want, the next step is to define their needs. Here we suggest you use the quality, time, cost/price and flexibility prompts that we have used in Figure 3.4 above. These prompts enable you to consider the customers' requirements, but you will have to be precise in defining them.

For example, your customers may say they are looking for a 'quality' product but what does that mean? A 'high quality' DVD recorder could be defined by any of the following:

- having a high specification (e.g. many features)
- being reliable
- having a well-known brand name
- being easy to use
- looking sleek and modern.

As you build your specification of the customers' requirements, you should be specific in your use of words.

A grumpy sales director During an early facilitation, a very grumpy sales director confronted me. I was trying to elicit the customers' requirements, so I asked:

'What do your customers want?'
'They want everything', was the reply.
'What do you mean?'
'They want high quality, they want it for nothing and they want it yesterday!'

> 'OK', I continued, 'so what happens when you answer the phone?'
>
> 'What do you mean?'
>
> 'Well, what is the first question your customer asks?'
>
> 'Do we have it in stock?', the sales director replied.
>
> 'So what do they do when you say "no"?'
>
> 'They put the phone down.'
>
> 'So availability of the product is their number one priority?'
>
> 'I see what you mean.'

As you work through your customer requirements, you will need to focus on what is most important to your customers. To do this we suggest you should differentiate between the 'order qualifiers' and order winners'.

- 'Order qualifiers' are the qualities your products and services must have as a minimum to be accepted in the market place.
- 'Order winners' are the qualities which your customers value and use when they decide whose products and services they are going to buy.

Qualifiers and winners In setting up the business to make windows, I had to obtain a BBA (British Board of Agreement) certificate to sell windows to builders in the new build market. Without this certificate, the windows would not meet the specification required. So this was an order qualifier. However, I did not win orders in this market by having a BBA certificate because all my competitors had one too. So the order winner was then around other factors, such as price and availability.

The key customer requirements you should be capturing in your discussions are the order winners, as you would be already on the verge of going out of business if the order qualifier criteria were not being met.

But order qualifiers and order winners change over time. In the 1960s, televisions were so unreliable that people rented their sets. Having a repair service was an order qualifier. However, the Japanese came along and made reliable televisions, which undermined the order qualifier. Over time they created a new qualifier – that television had to be reliable – and the rest is history!

One final point, if you have multiple customer requirements, as is seen in the brick example (Figure 3.4), then you should create a combined 'customer requirements' list before you embark on considering the requirements of your stakeholders. By merging the requirements that are the same, compromising on requirements that are similar and making decisions on those that conflict you can create the combined list.

How should you do this in practice? With multiple customers, we suggest you use Figure 3.4 to create the requirements. You will need to add a final right hand column, to create a combined list. You should then take this 'combined list' and copy it into the right hand column (customer needs) in Figure 3.3.

Similarly, you can take the same approach with your different stakeholders. Use Figure 3.4 for the different stakeholders. Then create a combined list, which summarises their requirements. Finally, copy this combined list into the right hand column (stakeholder needs) of Figure 3.3. But we will address the stakeholder fully in the next section.

Who are your stakeholders?

This is an important question. For most commercial organisations, the main stakeholders will include:

- Owners or shareholders – who want a return on their investment.
- Staff – who may want secure employment, fair rewards, safe working conditions and personal development.
- Suppliers – who may want stable demand, a fair price to be paid on time and a customer who is 'easy to deal with'.
- Regulators – who will want you to comply with their rules and the law.
- The local community – who may be concerned that your business will ruin their environment and way of life.

You may consider that some of these stakeholders are not very important. But let us look at a couple of examples:

- The local community – take the example of a small manufacturing company located in a village. The company wanted to expand its factory but the local community objected to the planning application. Permission was rejected, even though the plans appeared reasonable. Could this have been avoided if more consideration had been given to developing a good relationship with local people at an earlier stage?
- The regulator – a maggot farmer was asked to sit on the committee that set the standards for the industry. The government wanted to impose some regulations, but the farmer saw it as a commercial opportunity. By co-opting his friends onto the committee, he created a standard that suited his business, forcing many of his competitors to comply or leave the industry.

How do you determine their needs?

Members of the management team may well know the answer to this question, but you could meet your stakeholders and ask them directly what they want of your organisation. That is useful because assumptions about needs can be misleading.

In this process you can use the prompts of 'quality, time, cost/price and flexibility', but you will have to be more liberal in the interpretation of the prompts than you were with your customers.

Interestingly, the needs of the owners are often the least understood. Even the subsidiaries of parent companies rarely understand the requirements of their parent company (see the example below).

Return on capital employed When working with a high technology film manufacturer, I reached the stage of discussing the parent company's needs.

'A higher return on capital employed', came the assured answer.

But I wasn't sure. The parent company was investing very heavily in new plant and equipment and the returns were going to be disastrous for the next few years, so I challenged the response. As we argued back and forth it emerged that the subsidiary was the main supplier of film for the whole group, who then used the film in the products sold to the customer. This insight prompted a real dialogue with the parent company about their role in the group and their owners' objectives for them.

How do you reconcile stakeholders' needs and customers' needs?

Give a thought for the public sector   For a company, reconciling customer and stakeholder needs can be difficult, but give a thought for the public sector. A hospital might be faced with the following situations:

- Patients want privacy.
- Staff, who are busy, want to move easily from patient to patient as quickly as possible. Opening and closing doors detracts from this.
- For efficiency, staff need to supervise several patients at the same time. This can be achieved more easily in an open ward.
- The hospital management wants to fit in as many beds as possible into the space available.
- The government wants to cut waiting lists and also ensure patients have the best possible experience when they are in hospital.

Some of these stakeholder needs are at odds with each other. Dividing wards into separate rooms would militate against making best use of the space. The discussion would have to begin with understanding why patients wanted their own rooms. Do they simply want a screen between beds? Is it a question of noise and not being able to sleep at night? Are they looking for en suite facilities? If the last two statements were true then adding permanent screens rather than curtains would be unlikely to increase patient satisfaction, although it would afford more privacy.

There is no simple way to do this. It has to be done by discussion and agreeing priorities. Sometimes it is possible to compromise, sometimes difficult decisions have to be made. Remember, the discussion itself is a useful exercise in helping to define and agree what is really important for the organisation and what can and cannot be done.

Examining the needs of stakeholders is a useful exercise because it brings to the surface some of the contradictions and conflicts, Even if these cannot be reconciled entirely, at least they will be understood and possibly some compromises made. Sometimes discussion leads to turning down a particular course of action because, although it is attractive in itself, it sits uncomfortably when seen alongside the other plans. Reconciling needs can be about saying 'no'.

If you have developed the customer and stakeholder requirements from the customer, stakeholder objective sheet (Figure 3.3), then you will need to compare, balance and blend the two lists into a single set of objectives which meet the requirements of both the customer and the stakeholders. Figure 3.5 shows an example.

Some of these needs will obviously match. The customer may need high product reliability to minimise the inconvenience when the product goes wrong. The company may well have the same objective to minimise warranty costs. Here there is no conflict.

Some of these needs will appear at first sight to conflict. Customers may be looking for quick delivery. The company may want to meet return on investment (ROI) targets. Reducing stock levels may be seen as critical to achieving this. The customers' need for quick delivery and the stock reduction objective may therefore conflict. As a consequence, one of the resulting objectives may be to drastically reduce production lead-times.

Figure 3.5 shows an example of how the customer and stakeholder needs described above are translated into business objectives.

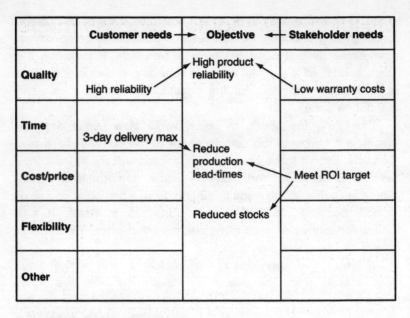

Figure 3.5: Developing business objectives

In this way a top-level set of organisational objectives are developed which meet both the customer needs and the needs of the stakeholders.

The final step

Depending on the complexity of your organisation, it will take one or two half-day workshops to develop the list of business objectives from your customer and stakeholder requirements. The last step is to create the success map, which will take an additional workshop.

Using the business objectives you have already identified, it should be relatively straightforward to use the 'what? / how?' process. You should also test what you create using the 'why' question.

Building stakeholder success maps

The third approach to deciding what to measure is a combination of the two approaches above. Some organisations have developed multiple success maps. Borealis (the Danish plastics company) created a success map for the business, together with a success map for its employees. They believed the employees were so important, that they needed to create a separate success map to represent how the company would deliver on this dimension (see Figure 3.6).

We are not recommending that you necessarily create and keep separate success maps for each of the stakeholders, but it is a useful approach as part of the process of creating the Balanced Scorecard.

The problem with the 'what? / how?' approach is that it is internally facing. When you use it you will find that you doesn't naturally take into account the requirements of the customer and other stakeholders. To overcome this problem, you should create a success map for each of the stakeholders in turn and then fuse them together to form a single success map. Taking this approach often gives useful insights and raises issues not surfaced by other methods.

What is the process for creating multiple stakeholder success maps?

We would suggest you adopt the following process:

1. Agree who are the stakeholders who have an interest in your business.
2. Identify the most important stakeholders whose requirements you wish to take into consideration when building your Balanced Scorecard.
3. Identify the key requirements of each of the stakeholders you have selected in turn. You can use the prompts from

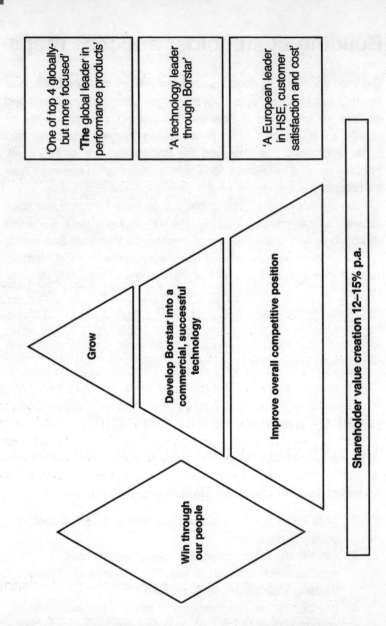

Figure 3.6: An example of multiple success maps

Figure 3.3 to do this, and you should focus on the order winners, rather than the order qualifiers. These requirements should form the 'whats?' at the top of your success map.

4. Apply the 'what? / how?' process to create the rest of the success map.

5. Validate the success map by asking the 'why?' question working up from the bottom.

6. Repeat steps 3 to 5 for all the stakeholders you identified in step 2. At the end of this process you will have a success map for each of the important stakeholders.

7. Finally, you should blend the individual stakeholder success maps into a single success map.

The last stage is quite difficult to do in practice. You should start by identifying the key overlaps, as these are usually substantial. However, you will have to make compromises and tough decisions when there is a conflict of interest. You will need to ensure the team is involved in this process, or at least get the opportunity to critique what you have done on their behalf.

In practice this approach looks more complicated than it is. In developing a Balanced Scorecard for part of the London Underground we identified some 22 stakeholders. Those with common interests were then grouped and we created eight stakeholder success maps. The whole process to arrive at the final single success map was achieved in four half-day meetings. This generated great debate and new insights for the team.

Conclusion

We have presented three alternative approaches for developing business objectives.

Each approach is different, but at their core they have aspects in common.

- They are all participative workshop approaches that involve and engage the whole senior management team.
- They all structure the discussion.
- They all encourage debate of the key issues.
- They are all simple and understandable techniques.
- They all lead to agreement on the key objectives to be met.

We believe the process of debate, understanding and agreement is the most important aspect of any strategy development or Balanced Scorecard design process. As we have already said, you can't delegate this to a staff team. The understanding and commitment to the decisions being made and the scorecard being developed only comes from being involved. If the senior management team feel it is not important enough for them to invest their time, then the rest of the business will quickly pick up that it is not important to the business either.

INSTANT TIP

Building success maps bringing together key people in your organisation, clarifies strategy and communicates successes.

04

How do you design appropriate measures?

Introduction

The previous chapter examined how to decide what you should measure. In this chapter we will look at how you measure it. You will learn how to construct an effective measure with a template – the performance measure record sheet – and provide examples of the type of questions you should ask. We examine the behavioural impact of measures and provide some tests of an effective measure with examples of good and bad practice. We end the chapter by suggesting a process for using the performance measure record sheet in your own organisation.

Why are measures important?

Success maps may create the structure for a performance measurement system, but it is the measures themselves that influence behaviour. Here are some examples of how important that can be.

Saving lives at sea   We were in conversation with a former member of the coastguard in the United States. For many years, the key measure for his organisation was the number of boat owners fined for not complying with safety requirements. However, it was agreed there should be a review of the key objectives and related measures. During this discussion someone pointed out that fining boat owners was not really what the coastguard service was all about. The ultimate aim was to save lives. As a result, the key performance indicator became the number of fatalities in the coastal waters under their control. These had been running fairly consistently at 90 per year. When the performance indicator was changed, the number of deaths at sea dropped to under 40!

Fighting crime   In a recent training session we were helping a group of senior police officers develop meaningful measures for their force. One group decided to create a measure for targeting a reduction in the number of murders committed. On reviewing the measure, it came to light that this was not currently a key measure. The force itself was targeted on reducing the total number of crimes committed. Hence, the theft of a mobile phone had the same weight as a murder. We challenged the officer proposing the measure on murder reduction and asked him what effect this could have. He claimed the current figure could be reduced by about 30 per cent. How? By paying particularly close attention to instances of domestic violence.

So performance measurement can cost lives. In the first example, refocusing effort significantly changed the way the coastguard acted resulting in fewer deaths at sea. In the second example, the impact is much more subtle. The key measure influences behaviour and directs the allocation of resources. No one wants higher murder rates, but when police forces are measured on overall crime numbers they will pursue activities that deliver that goal.

But even when lives are not at stake, measures can easily cause problems.

Problems with measures

Baggage delays An airline was concerned that an important aspect of customer satisfaction was determined not by the quality of service on the flight itself but by how quickly the passengers received their luggage after landing. As a result the company set as one of their objectives an improvement in baggage delivery speed. They introduced a performance measure in order to support their new initiative.

After this performance measure was introduced, a team of baggage handlers was observed in action at the airport. They were seen standing around chatting in a group awaiting the tractor pulling the baggage carts from the aeroplane. As the tractor arrived, the team leader sprang into action. He grabbed a small bag off the first car and threw it to the youngest member of the team, who caught the bag and sprinted across the tarmac. On reaching the baggage conveyor, he threw on the bag and hit the 'on' button. The bag disappeared in solitary splendour. He then relaxed, sauntering back to the rest of the group. All the other baggage handlers were unmoved by this frenetic activity and continued their conversation. It was only some minutes later that the whole team started to unload the carts.

So, what had caused this unfortunate behaviour? The measure selected by the company to improve delivery time of baggage centred on the time it took for the first bag to reach the conveyor. A change in behaviour did result – but it was not the change that had been intended!

The large nail   There is another (possibly apocryphal) example of a company producing nails in the former Soviet Union. They were set a target for manufacturing a given total tonnage of nails in that year. So what did they do? They created one enormous nail weighing the requisite amount but which was of no practical use to anyone! They had, however, fulfilled their annual target.

Clear thinking is vital when deciding what and how to measure. When taken at face value, some measures seem eminently suitable. But when followed to their logical conclusion, they make no sense at all. The key questions to ask are:

1. Is the measure really measuring what you want? (i.e. are cause and effect linked?)

   As a simple example of this: a training company wished to increase its profitability and decided a good indicator of future profitability would be the increase in numbers attending its open courses. What was the result? Profitability actually decreased because the manager responsible offered a series of 'cheap and cheerful' events that attracted large numbers of delegates but made no money. Increase in volume of sales does not always equal increase in profitability.

   and

2. What behaviour will the measure encourage? Is this behaviour desirable? (Think about the example of the baggage handlers.)

The performance measure record sheet

This sheet was developed by Professor Andy Neely and his colleagues at Cambridge University and has since been used by thousands of managers in many different types of organisation. The record sheet contains a series of simple questions. This provides a means by which you can think through and record each measure. It also brings consistency to your process.

The record sheet will help in a number of ways:

1. In establishing position, it will:
   - fully document the measure so everyone knows precisely how it is calculated
   - set out the frequency of measurement
   - name the person responsible for measuring
   - identify the source of data so the measure will be consistent over time; an important point if results are to be compared between two periods.

2. It will help in communicating direction by:
   - explaining why something is being measured
   - connecting performance measures to top level objectives, making a clear link
   - defining precisely what is to be achieved and by when.

3. It will help in aligning action to strategy by:
   - linking the measure to the objective is the success map
   - clearly articulating through the formula what is to be achieved.

4. It will help in stimulate action by:
   - naming the person responsible for ensuring performance improves
   - outlining the first steps in making an improvement.

We have already seen examples of how measures influence behaviour, and finally, the discussion arising from agreeing how to complete the record sheet should enable you and your team to learn and gain insights into how your organisation works.

Measure	A good self explanatory title
Purpose	Why are we measuring this?
Relate to	To which top level business object does this relate?
Target	What is to be achieved and by when?
Formula	How is this measured? Be precise.
Frequency	How often is this measured and reviewed?
Who measures?	Who collects and reports the data?
Source of data	Where does the data come from?
Who acts on the data?	Who is responsible for taking action?
What do they do?	What are the general steps which should be taken?
Notes and comments	

Figure 4.1: The performance measure record sheet (Adapted from Neely et al, 1996)

What should be included in the record sheet?

Title

It is very important that the title captures the essence of the measure. Financial measures can be clear (e.g. return on capital employed) but a measure simply called 'customer service' could relate to 'customer complaints', 'on time delivery', 'customer satisfaction surveys' or a whole basket of requirements. Try to be precise as well as concise. What constitutes a 'customer complaint'? Is it an email, phone call or just a little grumble to a salesperson?

What is the purpose?

Why is this being measured? If you cannot come up with a good reason, then think again whether this is really a good measure. Think: 'What behaviour will this encourage and is that behaviour desirable?'

What does the measure relate to?

Measures should support the achievement of top-level objectives. Managers are often inclined to insert measures that will show them or their team in a good light, rather than directly linking them to the organisation's objectives. Linking the measure to a top-level business objective makes this more difficult to do. It also makes sure resources are being directed to the areas most likely to yield results.

What is the target?

What performance target should be set? Your target should be realistic and achievable but also provide some 'stretch' to encourage a higher level of performance. The temptation is always to set a target that is easily achieved so there is no risk of failure. Every target needs a time frame in which it is to be reached.

What is the formula?

How is the performance measure to be calculated? Many mistakes have been made in companies where the method of calculating the formula has been left to the IT department who have selected a means of measurement based on the easiest and quickest method, rather than thinking what they are really measuring. On the other hand, it is no use selecting a formula when you have no chance of getting the source data. (Many managers complain about an overload of management information and statistics. This is a good test of whether you have the right data and information.)

How often should I measure?

Different measures require different intervals between measurement. Using the customer complaint example, in some high volume businesses it may be important to measure these weekly. In others, a monthly or bi-monthly measurement may suffice.

Who measures?

It is important to allocate responsibility to an individual rather than to a large team where responsibility could become unclear.

What is the source of the data?

This should be specified so the measure is taken consistently.

Who takes action?

Again, allocate responsibility to an individual (even if that person is responsible for or working on behalf of a team).

What should they do?

Under this heading specify in outline the types of action, which could be taken to improve performance against this measure. If this cannot be done, does this mean the factor you are measuring is beyond your control? You could, for example, take action on the number of people who have accidents on your premises but would have little control over absences caused by accidents outside work (other than employ more careful people, of course!).

Notes and comments

This is a space to record any additional notes and comments and is a useful aid for helping the process. For example, if your target was more or less a guess rather than being based on evidence from past performance, you might want to note this and review the target again at an appropriate point. If there was disagreement about how the attribute should be measured, then it is useful to note this and review the measure again at a suitable period after it has been implemented.

Pitfalls to avoid

But just take care when designing measures. People are very conscious of how they are to be measured. They often resist being measured on factors that they haven't been measured on before. Why is this? Because it is new, because they do not have the experience of delivering on this new measure and because the initial target may be arbitrary as there is no history to build on.

I'm good at it! Some time ago, I created a performance measurement system for a privately owned manufacturing company. The whole thrust of the new direction lay in being more flexible and responsive to the customer. Having created a set of objectives that reflected this new direction; the directors went away to develop the measures.

I met up with the operations director a couple of weeks later to review his proposal before the next board meeting and we went through the performance measure record sheet together.

The measure he had selected was 'overall equipment effectiveness', in other words, how long he ran his machines. My immediate reaction was 'how does this relate to being more responsive to customers?', but we pressed on with the process of completing the record sheet.

The next box was 'purpose': why are we measuring this? He answered that it was all to do with overhead recovery and machine utilisation. By now I was getting worried. The third question was 'to which objective does this measure relate?' Here he paused, and then confidently stated, 'profit'. I had to explain that the finance director was creating a measure of profit. The objective he was trying to develop a measure for was 'increasing operational responsiveness'. A heated argument ensued, but we eventually developed a measure around reducing product lead-times.

When we had finally finished, I asked why he had chosen 'overall equipment effectiveness'? His reply was 'because I am good at it!'

The example above has real implications for designing performance measures, as we need to develop measures for activities the organisation needs to be good at, rather than measures for activities the individual is already good at.

Measures are used for reporting performance up the organisation. This can be dangerous if the wrong information is reported or the wrong inferences taken.

Negotiating with the boss Some years ago, I set up a subsidiary company of a building materials group making windows. This was developed from a green field site in Corby, sourcing the machine tools from Belgium, recruiting a new team from both within the parent company and elsewhere. One afternoon, very early in the process I was sitting in my office when an email came in from my boss, Brian, who was the group managing director. We were in a particularly bad state as we had just found a crack in the factory floor and we had to repair it. The machine tools were late arriving from Belgium and my sales manager was still sorting out a problem in his old job with the sister company before he joined us.

In his email, Brian asked me to provide him with the value of our invoiced sales on a weekly basis from now on. The problem was that we didn't have any weekly sales and I didn't want him to have a sheet of paper every week with a string of zeros on it. So I invented a second column – the value of our order intake. But as soon as I had done that, I realised that we didn't have any orders either, so I had to invent a third column – the value of our quotations made. At last we had a non-zero figure to report as we had just quoted my friend Jurgen for £250,000 of windows for a project in Eastern Germany. This was a project we eventually won but never started, as they didn't have the finances to pay for the windows.

So this was my negotiation with my boss about what he wanted to know and what I wanted to tell him. Many years later, I realised that I had been particularly astute in my choice of information to provide. Brian was an accountant and what I had designed was a set of leading financial indicators to which he could readily relate.

However, some three months later, Brian rang me one Friday morning to give me a pep talk and tell me how well he thought we were doing. I really didn't see how he could be so positive; as the machine tool delays and the floor resurfacing had put us back a long way. But finally, my curiosity meant I really couldn't help but ask Brian why he thought we were doing so well.

'Well you know that tick sheet you send me every Friday afternoon', he started, and I immediately realised that he did read it, 'For every week this month you have had a non-zero number in every column.'

I came off the telephone very pleased and walked round to my customer services manager, Peter, to tell him the news.

'And how are we doing this week?' I asked.

'This is the last week of the month, so we are despatching and invoicing like mad. The enquiries are coming in so our quotation value is good.'

'But what about the orders?', I asked.

'None so far', was his reply.

I went in search of my sales manager Geoff who was sitting in the office and I quickly filled him in on my telephone conversation with Brian. When I asked about the possibility of an order his reply was rather disappointing:

'It's the last day of the month', he said, 'no one is gong to place an order now before Monday morning.'

'But what about Brian?', I replied, 'we will break our perfect record for the month!'

Geoff looked dejected, but then he suddenly said:

'Ah, Chris [one of our sales reps] wants his top floor windows doing on his house.'

'Great', I said, but if he wants a good price, today is the last day he is going to get it.'

So we took the order and maintained our perfect record for the month.

But what was I really doing? I simply responded to the performance measures I was being judged against and like many others, adjusted my behaviour to deliver what was being measured.

Examples of record sheets

The following two examples come from a training company who, in discussing success factors for their business, realised their reputation lay largely in the hands of their many associate tutors. Ensuring these people were up to date in the knowledge of their subject suddenly seemed of utmost importance. However, it was difficult to encourage the tutors to undertake formal training and development themselves as it took up their fee earning time. Therefore, a measure was introduced to encourage tutors to provide feedback on their own personal development.

Measure	Updating associate tutors' knowledge.
Purpose	To maintain and improve the quality of the courses and protect the reputation of the company.
Relates to	Ensuring associate tutors have up-to-date knowledge of their subject.
Target	100 per cent of tutors have updated their knowledge.
Formula	$\dfrac{\text{Number of tutors who have provided acceptable evidence}}{\text{Total number of associate tutors.}} \times 100$
Frequency	Six monthly.
Who measures?	Jane Bishop, HR Training Executive.
Source of data	Six-monthly tutor returns.
Who acts on data?	Gill Robertson, Programme Director.
What do they do?	Assess the quality of the returns, checking all have been received; follow up on tutors who have not provided a return or insufficient evidence of updating knowledge; take steps to remove tutors where appropriate.
Notes and comments	The tutors' handbook will provide examples of appropriate updating activities.

The training company also needed to attract new customers to their events in order to grow sales, but there was a concern that the business development managers should also maintain relationships with existing customers. The decision was taken to count the delegates sent on courses by new customers. But how should 'new customers' be that defined. It was decided that 'new customers' would be those who had not bought before the start of the financial year as this would encourage the business development managers to pursue repeat business with new customers rather than just getting them to book delegates for a one-off event.

Measure	Level of new business on open programmes.
Purpose	To attract new customers.
Relates to	Growing the business.
Target	30 per cent of course delegates from new customers.
Formula	$$\frac{\text{Number of bookings per course from new customers}}{\text{Number of attendees per course.}} \times 100$$
Frequency	Monthly.
Who measures?	Gill Deakin, Programme Director.
Source of data	Booking database.
Who acts on data?	Gill Deakin, Programme Director.
What do they do?	Discuss performance with the Business Development Managers and agree tactics for improvement.
Notes and comments	A new customer is a company that has not purchased before this financial year.

Examples of common measures

The following are commonly chosen measures representing each perspective of the Balanced Scorecard.

Financial – return on capital employed (ROCE)

When using this measure to manage the business, the accounting accuracy is less important than understanding the impact the measure will have on behaviour. But it is important to be clear about how it will be calculated and ensure it will always be calculated in a consistent way.

The outcome you probably want from this measure is that your company increases its return on capital employed either by earning greater profits or by more efficient use of that capital. This will encourage your management team to increase sales, reduce costs and manage their working capital efficiently. However, the disadvantages are that it might also encourage them to take some easier options such as delaying capital investment, damaging long-term efficiencies or postponing research and development projects which are unlikely to result in a quick return. They might also reduce marketing and sales expenditure, which could have a detrimental effect in the long term. All these undesirable tactics will have the result of improving your return on capital employed.

The Balanced Scorecard helps to overcome some of these difficulties by including other measures, such as new product development, that counteract the tendency to choose some of these tactics that cause damage in the longer term.

The following is a straightforward example of a measure for a small growing business whose senior team is concerned to get value from their recent investment in new machinery

Measure	Return on capital employed.
Purpose	To ensure adequate returns are being made from capital employed.
Relates to	The need for the business to make sufficient return for its investors.
Target	Achieve a rate of return of over 20 per cent within three years.
Formula	$\dfrac{\text{Profit before tax and interest}}{\text{Net capital employed}} \times 100$
Frequency	Measured monthly; reviewed quarterly.
Who measures?	Chris Millington, Finance Director.
Source of data	Monthly management accounts.
Who acts on data?	Ashok Kotecha, Sales Director; Georgina Simons, Operations Director.
What do they do?	Ensure optimum machine set up; review sales volumes and margins; manage stock levels.
Notes and comments	

External – customer complaints

Most businesses record and analyse customer complaints. Although few people enjoy dealing with complaints, they provide a good means of learning what is happening so corrective action can be taken. It is far worse to lose customers who switch supplier without letting you know why. However, staff can be reluctant to record complaints, particularly if they fear being blamed or see complaints as a nuisance and an interruption to their work. So the way in which action is taken as a result of this measure is particularly sensitive. If there is a serious problem in performance which is the cause of complaints then that must be dealt with, but heavy-handedness will simply result in complaints being swept under the carpet, whatever process is in place to try to prevent this from happening.

Measure	Customer complaints.
Purpose	To understand what upsets customers so service and products can be improved.
Relates to	Satisfying customers and retaining their business in the future.
Target	Maintaining a customer complaint level of under 5 per cent per annum.
Formula	$\dfrac{\text{Number of customer complaints}}{\text{Number of orders despatched}} \times 100$
Frequency	Monthly.
Who measures?	Julie Carter, Customer Service Manager.
Source of data	Customer complaints system.
Who acts on data?	Julie Carter, Customer Service Manager.
What do they do?	Analyse complaints by type, ensure relevant managers are informed of problems in their area and that those managers report back corrective action taken. Flag any major trends for discussion at quarterly management meeting.
Notes and comments	A customer complaint is an email, letter or problem highlighted by telephone call to call centre staff which is logged on to the complaints system.

There is a further question: what is a complaint? Is it an email, letter or just a mention during a telephone call or sales visit. The definition will depend on the type of business and customer relationships but clear definition is necessary.

Internal process – first time yield

First time yield is a term used in manufacturing to describe the amount of good quality product produced by a process at the first attempt. It is important because scrap is wasteful and expensive, rework to rectify mistakes costs money and inconsistencies in first time yield can cause planning problems leading to uncertain delivery and customer dissatisfaction. There are many benefits of measuring first time yield. However, it can be difficult to collect the data; particularly in ensuring all rework is measured and all the processes are included in the measure. Here is an example from a maker of uPVC windows.

Measure	First time yield.
Purpose	To measure the rate of improvement in production efficiency.
Relates to	The need to reduce waste, minimise rework and reduce costs.
Target	Achieve a first time yield rate of 95 per cent.
Formula	$\dfrac{\text{Number of finished units at first attempt}}{\text{Number of units processed}} \times 100$
Frequency	Monthly.
Who measures?	Mark Proudfoot, Production Manager.
Source of data	Daily process record sheets.
Who acts on data?	Nigel Lermon, Production Controller.
What do they do?	Ensure causes for failure are analysed and corrective action taken and impact reviewed.
Notes and comments	We need to monitor the impact of the new operator training initiative planned for July on the results of this measure.

Innovation and learning

Innovation and learning can be difficult to measure as it is usually intangible. However, most businesses remain ahead of their competitors by learning from what they are doing and using what they have learnt. The following is an example from a firm of consultants who were concerned to find from their time sheets that highly paid consultants were spending a great deal of time producing presentations for their clients. Managing partners were also noticing how similar some of the material was when they accompanied their team members at presentations. They decided to set up a 'presentations' database where consultants could store re-usable parts of their presentations and record feedback they received from their clients on those presentations. The two measures below were used to encourage use of and contributions to that database.

Measure	Use of existing knowledge.
Purpose	To encourage consultants to use existing knowledge rather than always re-inventing it.
Relates to	Consultants' efficiency.
Target	50 per cent of client presentations incorporate existing knowledge
Formula	$\dfrac{\text{Number of presentations using database material}}{\text{Number of client presentations}} \times 100$
Frequency	Monthly.
Who measures?	Jo Watson, Knowledge Manager.
Source of data	Presentations database.
Who acts on data?	Sector Heads.
What do they do?	Identify teams who are not using existing knowledge and discuss reasons for not using existing material.
Notes and comments	

Measure	Presentation resource development.
Purpose	To encourage consultants to share work they have done on developing client presentations.
Relates to	Consultants' efficiency and learning.
Target	Appropriate material included from 100 per cent of client presentations.
Formula	$$\frac{\text{Number of presentations where material is put on database}}{\text{Number of client presentations}} \times 100$$
Frequency	Monthly.
Who measures?	Jo Watson, Knowledge Manager.
Source of data	Presentations database.
Who acts on data?	Sector Heads.
What do they do?	Identify teams not contributing to the database and discuss reasons for this.
Notes and comments	

Designing survey-based measures

So far, most of this chapter has been focused on designing internal measures of performance. These are produced from information we have within the organisation, with the data often being extracted from our computer systems. On occasions such measures are rather blunt instruments. They only reflect our view of the world and do not reflect external perception.

Why does perception matter?

Companies typically measure many attributes of their customer offering. There are measures of 'on-time delivery', service quality, speed of response, invoicing accuracy and so on. All these measures come from the organisation's own databases, so we know what our performance was (according to these measures) but we do not know if the customer was satisfied. To complete the picture we need to establish the customers' perception. For the customer, perception is reality and this is not the same as your internal performance measures. Let us take a couple of examples.

As consumers, we all buy products that are very similar, but some are more expensive than others. Take BMWs: they are the same size and weight as many of their competitors, but you pay a premium to buy a BMW. There may well be technical differences in performance, but part of the premium comes from people simply perceiving that BMWs are better cars.

Interestingly, perception also holds true for industrial customers. Buyers may have access to great swathes of information on your performance as a supplier, but until their perception changes, you may find it difficult to make a sale.

Milliken's customer satisfaction Milliken is a manufacturer of industrial fibres. For many years now they have measured customer satisfaction and Clive Jeanes, their former European managing director, told a story about how they learnt a very important lesson about the link between internal company measures and customer perception.

The European division embarked on a programme to increase on-time delivery of their product to customers. Over a period, they improved this considerably and were looking forward to the results of the annual customer satisfaction survey. When the results arrived, they were surprised. Although their internal measure showed that Milliken was now amongst the best in their class, the customer satisfaction with on-time delivery hardly moved at all. They asked their customers why this was so, and the response was:

'You tell us when our goods will be delivered, but, in fact, that is the date you despatch the goods from your factory, so we always receive the goods late.'

So Milliken improved their internal performance measure from 'despatched on-time' to 'delivered on-time'. This required additional work, and after a dip in performance, the company developed systems that performed well. But again, this was not reflected in the annual customer satisfaction survey.

What was the problem now? The customers reported back:

'You tell us when we can have the product, but this isn't when we want it. If we ask for six weeks delivery and your standard lead time is 12 weeks, there is no flexibility.'

So Milliken went away again and re-engineered their operation to deal with this issue. They changed their on-time measure to reflect the negotiated date. This wasn't always the date the customer originally requested, but was the date agreed after discussions and usually reflected the customers' need. Now, Milliken had a real challenge to deliver on this new measure. They also realised there were other characteristics of a 'perfect order'. The delivery had to be the complete quantity ordered, the delivery note had to be correct and the invoice had to be right. So the 'on-time delivery' measure was redesigned to take all these factors into account.

After months of hard work, Milliken was pleased when their customer satisfaction survey showed an improvement in perception of 'on-time delivery'. But when they reflected on what they were achieving, they realised that although their performance was outstanding, customer satisfaction didn't reflect this. One plant, LeHavre, went for over six years without a late delivery, but customer satisfaction with 'on-time delivery' didn't reflect this.

When they presented this new problem to their customers, they were again surprised at the response. The customers simply didn't perceive that they had a problem with 'on-time delivery' from Milliken, so they scored them as good rather than excellent – which they would have expected after all their hard work.

Milliken's solution was a good one. The sales executives were asked to drop into the conversation with their customers how long it had been since they had had a late delivery. The sales executives in Le Havre took great pleasure in reminding their customers that every order had been delivered on time for the last six years.

It was this action that moved Milliken's satisfactions score from good to excellent.

The message of this story is that perception and hard performance measures are not the same. You need to measure perception as that drives buying behaviour. But you cannot measure perception too often as this results in 'survey fatigue'. However, you can measure your own performance much more regularly. This allows you to direct your employees and track progress, but always compare this internal measure with the customers' perception as it proves a great opportunity for new insights and learning.

Sometimes, perception is all that is available, especially in service operations. Take a restaurant as an example. How do you measure the quality of service? You can film the restaurant staff and the get an experienced person to evaluate and score the service, but this is expensive, time consuming and you can only sample what is happening occasionally. A much simpler way is to ask your customer for feedback.

We are focusing on customer satisfaction, but the same points can be applied to employee satisfaction or the perception of other stakeholders. But let us now look at how you design the measure itself.

How do you design a customer satisfaction measure?

There is a simple answer. Create a scale – for example, very dissatisfied, dissatisfied, neutral, satisfied, very satisfied – and then ask one question.

'Overall, how satisfied are you with XYZ Ltd as a supplier.'

This gives a response you can turn into a measure that you report back to the organisation. You can use the performance measure record sheet to complete the design of the measure in the way we described earlier in this chapter.

How do you set a target for customer satisfaction?

Earlier in this chapter, we discussed how the way in which measures are designed can affect behaviour. This is also true for survey measures and the way you set the target has a big influence on how people react. In setting the target, the question you must ask is:

'What behaviour do we want from our employees?'

Let us illustrate this with some examples using the scale we described above.

Very dissatisfied	Dissatisfied	Neutral	Satisfied	Very satisfied
1	2	3	4	5

By giving each response a point weighting you can calculate an average customer satisfaction score from adding up all the points and dividing by the number of responding customers (ideally, you should also check for non-respondent bias by asking some of those not responding to the survey for their scores to ensure they are similar to those who had responded).

If you do this, you can calculate that the overall customer satisfaction is, say, 3.6. This may not mean anything on its own, but if you repeat the survey, you can see if it has increased or decreased since last year. You can then set a target to improve customer satisfaction to '4' over the next two years.

Our holiday We had a lovely holiday in Grenada a few years ago. When we came to pay the bill at the end of our week the receptionist asked:

'Did you have a good holiday?
'Wonderful!', Pippa replied.
'Would you complete our customer satisfaction survey for us?', the receptionist continued without taking breath.

Bias can easily creep in if you allow staff to select the respondents in this way. This is the reason most airlines designate the seat number of the passenger they want to

> complete the survey rather than leaving the choice to the cabin crew. But even this can be fiddled with a complimentary bottle of champagne!

Remember, there are there ways of setting targets and these should be chosen based on the situation the company is in and the response you want from your staff. For example, you can set the targets as follows (see also Table 1):

1. Increase our very satisfied customer response to over 50 per cent. This will focus staff attention on moving satisfied customers to being very satisfied.
2. Increase the percentage of satisfied customers to over 80 per cent. This will focus people on ensuring a good standard of service, but probably not on 'delighting the customer'.
3. Ensure that over 95 per cent of customers are not dissatisfied. This focuses effort towards removing sources of dissatisfaction.
4. Reduce our very dissatisfied customers to less than 2 per cent. Now you are focusing on managing complaints, providing service recovery if things go wrong, pacifying customers with financial compensation, or even trying to remove very dissatisfied customers from the customer list!

One final point, research has shown that those 'very satisfied' are five to six times more likely to buy again from you than those who are only 'satisfied' and if you consider the cost of finding a new customer compared with keeping an existing customer, you will rapidly appreciate the 'top box'.

	Very Dissatisfied	Dissatisfied	Neutral	Satisfied	Very satisfied
1					50% Very Satisfied
2				80% satisfied	
3			95% Not dissatisfied		
4	2% Very dissatisfied				

Table 1: A satisfaction scale

What is the difference between a survey and a measure?

Most simple questionnaires have six to eight questions and some of the airline customer satisfaction surveys go on for pages. But here we must differentiate between the measure and the survey. When you are measuring customer satisfaction, there is a whole set of questions you can ask about the product your customer has just bought, or the service they have just received. In a restaurant you can ask how satisfied they were with:

- reception by the Maitre d'
- efficiency of the waiter
- attentiveness of the waiter
- quality of the food
- presentation of the food
- extensiveness of the wine list
- ambience of the restaurant
- value for money of their experience.

Now all these are important factors that contribute to customer satisfaction, but they are not satisfaction itself. Some organisations want to add up the scores and then report the average, but we would advise against this for the following reasons:

1. Are the individual questions of equal importance? This is rarely the case, so if you are going to produce a score you need to weight the different components.
2. Weighting the elements makes the formula rather complicated. It may also add expense, as you need to ask the respondents to give their weightings. Finally, the results may not even be correct after all this effort.
3. You can use statistical techniques to investigate whether the overall satisfaction reflects the factors you have identified in the list.

For the measure, the single question is: 'How satisfied are you with ...?' The additional information just provides insights into what determines that level of satisfaction.

You must remember too that you are only surveying your existing customers when you measure customer satisfaction. Existing customers may be satisfied, that is why they are customers, but past customers may not have been and that is why they have left. When doing surveys, you may wish to look at the wider group and understand how non-customers perceive you. But that is about gathering information to guide decision-making rather than creating a measure of customer satisfaction.

One last point, in many customer satisfaction surveys there are two useful additional questions which many people use as measures in their own right.

1. Would you recommend our products / services to friends and colleagues?
2. Would you buy again?

Often, when you analyse your data you will find that customer satisfaction is not statistically significantly correlated with repeat purchases. The link tends to be that satisfaction leads to willingness to recommend, willingness to recommend leads to an indication that they would buy again, and this leads to repeat business. As a result, in some organisations, these two questions are used to create measures in their own rights, but you should check your own data to see if this holds for your organisation.

What is the process for designing the measures?

A large part of the value of completing the record sheet lies in the discussion it generates. The debate will often be lively, as people are naturally sensitive about how their performance, or the performance of their area of the business, is going to be measured. If there is little or no debate it is probably a sign that people are not engaging with the process and you will find that you have no commitment to implement the final set of measures.

We suggest that you should take the following approach:

1. Once the top-level business objectives have been agreed, you should divide the task of defining the performance measures between the management team.
2. Ask each manager to develop a measure using the performance measure record sheet for each of his or her objectives. They should be asked to involve members of their team where appropriate.
3. The manager involved in creating the success map will understand why the objective is important. Members of their team will be much more able to contribute to the design of the measure as they are closer to the day-to-day working of the company. Involving them also helps in the communication process.
4. The first measure will take 45 minutes to an hour to complete. Subsequent measures will require 30 to 45 minutes.

5. When this has been done, you will need to convene a workshop to review the performance measures. This workshop should comprise the senior management team who developed the success map.
6. You will need to review each measure in turn, accepting, modifying or rejecting these measures.
7. You should expect a large number of the measures to require modification or rework. If they do not, it is a sign the team is not taking the process seriously and the measures won't be implemented.
8. You will normally require a second workshop to finalise the measures and agree the implementation plan.

Conclusion

To get a good Balanced Scorecard you will need to combine:

1. The big picture of what the strategy is and how it will be delivered.
2. The detail design of the appropriate measures.

Chapter 3 focused on developing the big picture and the creation of the success maps. But, on their own, success maps are not sufficient. You need to get the measures right too.

In this chapter, we have emphasised the importance of creating 'good' measures. We have also shown you the consequences of getting the measures wrong. In the next chapter, we will address the thorny issue of implementation. How do you get all these measures implemented in your organisation?

INSTANT TIP

Get your measures right! Don't measure x and expect y.

05

How do you implement a Balanced Scorecard?

Introduction

We start this chapter by looking at why implementation of the Balanced Scorecard fails. This happens far more often than one would expect

We will give you a series of tools to conduct a pre-implementation assessment and then go on to describe a process to help you implement your scorecard. Finally, we will identify the main reasons why Balanced Scorecard projects fail, differentiating between the hurdles you can overcome, and the real show stoppers.

How often do Balanced Scorecard initiatives fail?

It has been claimed that 70 per cent of Balanced Scorecard initiatives fail. Why is that so? If you ask any group of managers to brainstorm a list of reasons, they will produce something akin to the list below:

- The company picks the wrong measures.
- The measures picked aren't relevant to those running the business.
- Targets set are unrealistic.
- The measures are not aligned with the goals.
- The system is too complex.
- The measures require too much effort to collect.
- People do not understand the system.
- Not enough time and effort is put into training and education.
- Poor project management.
- Lack of top management support.
- Initial enthusiasm wanes.
- IT support is inadequate.
- There is no performance review mechanism.
- Measures get out of date.
- Measures conflict with the reward system.
- Measures do not align with the appraisal system.
- Measures aren't used.
- Measures are resisted.
- The shift in power caused by the Balanced Scorecard is resisted.

The list always starts with issues concerning the Balanced Scorecard and the measures themselves, progresses to issues about understanding and time and effort and then focuses on top management support and the conflict with other systems. The issue about resistance and the shift in power that measurement can cause usually comes out at the end with a little prompting.

But what the list does show is that most people understand why initiatives such as the Balanced Scorecard fail. Yet managers continue to promote initiatives that go on to fail despite this knowledge.

So how can you make a Balanced Scorecard initiative succeed?

1. You should undertake an analysis of the situation so you understand the context for the Balanced Scorecard

implementation and can act on the results to maximise your chances of success.

2. You should use a robust process for implementation.

How do you analyse the situation?

There is a whole literature on change management, but here we will outline three techniques we have found useful in doing pre-assessments of scorecard implementations. These are:

● Force-field analysis
● Change responses
● Benefit/effort analysis.

We will now describe these in turn.

Force-field analysis

One of the oldest and most used techniques for analysing the resistance to change is force-field analysis. Force-field analysis is based on the premise that change will only occur if the forces driving the change are greater than the forces resisting the change. Constructing a force field analysis is a relatively easy exercise. You identify all the forces driving the change and write them down on the left hand side of a sheet of paper and identify and write all the forces blocking or resisting the change on the other. Against each force, you should draw an arrow. The length of the arrow should represent the strength of the force as you perceive it.

The result will appear similar to Figure 5.1. You can then use the diagram to assess whether the change is likely to be successful or not. You should also recognise the major forces for change, which have to be preserved, and the significant forces against change, which have to be counteracted.

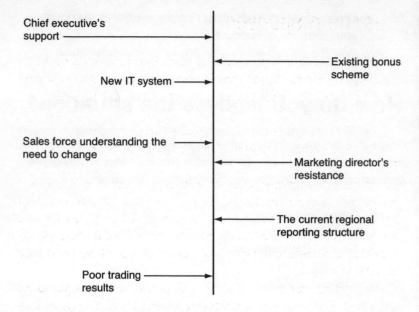

Figure 5.1: An example of a force-field analysis

The advantage of force-field analysis lies in its simplicity. It is quick to use and the results can easily be communicated to and understood by the implementation team. However, it does have shortcomings. Firstly, it is very subjective and relies on your (or a small group of your colleagues') assessment of the forces. Secondly, it assumes the Balanced Scorecard project will occur in isolation. In fact, most changes fail because they are simply overtaken by other projects or events, rather than as a result of a lack of support or resistance to change.

Change responses

Paul Strebel of IMD suggested that resistance to change could be assessed by considering the anticipated responses of those affected by the change. There are two dimensions you should consider:

● The energy of their response (active or passive)
● The perceived potential impact (positive or negative)

The impact of change is often clear to see, a loss of position and power for some individuals, but an opportunity for advancement and new opportunities for others. On the other hand, you will find the energy of response is less easy to identify as it depends on individuals' perceptions of the uncertainty of the change and their attitude to risk.

Using this approach, you should create four categories of individual: traditionalists, bystanders, resistors and change agents (see Figure 5.2).

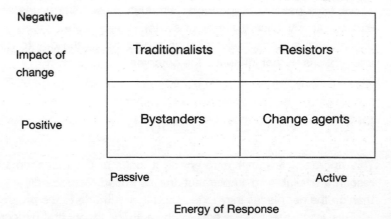

Figure 5. 2: The four change categories

To identify the individuals who fall into the different groups, you need to ask four questions:

1. Who is likely to respond actively to the change and see it as an opportunity? (change agents)
2. Who is likely to respond actively to the change and see it as a threat? (resistors)
3. Who is likely to respond passively to the change and see it as an opportunity? (bystanders)
4. Who is likely to respond passively to the change and see it as a threat? (traditionalists)

The advantage of using this tool is that it categorises those involved in the change into four distinct camps and suggests a variety of incentives that can be applied to increase the level of commitment to the change. It can also be used quickly to assess the position of those involved.

However, the technique relies on your subjective knowledge of the people involved, and your ability to be able to segregate the active from passive responders (although these differences will surface quickly once the project starts). It also assumes you are dealing with a single major change project so all the day-to-day interruptions do not influence the outcome.

Priority, effort and benefit

This approach is rather different as it looks at the management resource available to implement the Balanced Scorecard rather than on the people, as individuals, and their attitude to the project.

This assessment tool is built on the authors' theory that projects compete with each other for management time and attention. Therefore, whether a Balanced Scorecard implementation will succeed or not will depend on:

- the effort available
- the expected benefits the project is likely to bring
- the subsequent priority the project receives.

This has been shown to be the case in a study of actual Balanced Scorecard implementations and we found the approach is very effective in establishing whether or not a project is likely to succeed.

How do you use this tool?

Ideally, you should interview each of the managers and key individuals who are to be directly involved in the scorecard project and ask them:

1. What are the major improvement projects, which will occupy your time and effort over the next three to six months?
2. Would you please rank these projects in their order of importance, as you currently perceive it, by allocating 100 points between your improvement projects?
3. If you were given 100 points of your effort to split between these projects, how much of your effort would each project take to make reasonable progress over the next three to six months?
4. If all these projects take 100 points of effort, how much of your effort is required just to complete the day-to-day routine task of your job?
5. If the total points of effort for the projects and routine activities is (3+4), then what, in your opinion, is your total available effort?

This approach will allow you to:

1. Identify all the projects currently competing for management time and effort.

2. Produce an approximate ranking of the priority of the current projects, from the perspective of the different directors and managers involved.
3. Identify the level of support, which the scorecard project is receiving. This is revealed from its relative position in the ranking. This is important because if you ask managers for their support they will invariably reply 'yes'. But if you ask them to rank the priority, they will reveal their own preference without outwardly rejecting the scorecard project from the start.
4. Assess whether those involved are, or expect to be, overloaded by their day-to-day work or volume of improvement projects.

A worked example

It is useful to create a picture of the situation by drawing a diagram in the form of Figure 5.3. Figure 5.3 has been created from the data gathered through the interview described above and shown in the Table 5.1 below.

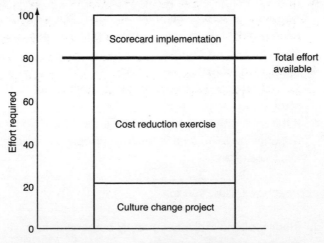

Figure 5.3: Graph of the managing director's improvement projects

Project descriptions		Improvement project effort
Rank		Required
50	Culture change project	30
30	Cost reduction exercise	50
20	Balanced scorecard implementation	20
	1. Total improvement project effort required	100
	2. Total effort required for everyday job	100
	3. Total effort required (1+2)	200
	4. Total effort available	180

Table 5.1: Interview responses, company managing director

Figure 5.3 shows that the culture change project currently has the highest priority, but that the managing director is not going to spend a great deal of effort on it. It also shows that, after taking into account the day to day demands of the job, the managing director considers he is overloaded and there should be concerns as to whether the Balanced Scorecard project is going to be completed or progress according to schedule.

A cuckoo in the nest We undertook a Balanced Scorecard pre-assessment project in a manufacturing company in the north of England. Several divisions of this company were taken through the process in parallel and all the managers involved were interviewed prior to the process.

One divisional general manager turned out to be against the process, but it was not obvious from the start. We found out afterwards that he had a habit of only bringing success stories to the management meetings. All his graphs would be going upwards! But that wasn't going to continue under the new Balanced Scorecard project. He had managed this in the past by selecting the improving measures to present at the meeting and deflecting attention away from things that weren't going well. The Balanced Scorecard project was going to regularise the meetings so that the same items would be on the agenda each time. Under the new regime, problem issues weren't going to be so easily hidden. We believe he felt threatened and so acted accordingly.

When we completed his chart, the general manger had seven specific improvement projects. The Balanced Scorecard project was his lowest priority. This in itself should have raised concerns. He also ranked it after a group marketing project he really wasn't involved with and was a project of no real consequence. But this too was not raised at the time as he claimed he had the resource available to undertake the Balanced Scorecard project.

When it came to the workshops, the general manager was rather reluctant to venture an opinion. Only occasionally, when riled by a barbed comment, did he show that he had a far greater understanding of how the business operated than he was portraying in the meeting. As a result, some of the discussions about the future of the business were impoverished, through his lack of input.

The general manager finally showed his hand in the last meeting, when he set the meeting up with a very effective joke about consultants. Then, at the perfect moment, he launched his attack, identified only a couple of benefits they would take forward from the project and effectively undermined all the work.

Could this have been identified in advance? I don't think we would have spotted his position from either a force-field analysis or from assessing his change response. We simply didn't understand that he was an active resistor, because we didn't realise he would see the Balanced Scorecard as a threat. The interview material gave some clues to his position and we would identify the problem in advance if this happened again.

Advantages and shortcomings

The advantage of using this tool is that it provides a way of assessing the potential success or failure of projects by asking those directly involved. It provides feedback in the form of priorities that can be used to identify potential problem areas.

The technique has one major benefit in that it does not directly ask whether the person being interviewed supports the project or not. It is much easier for managers to argue that other projects should have higher priority in their eyes and shows their resistance to a project by the position it is placed on the graph – often with lowest priority.

The approach does have a shortcoming in that it requires the nature of the project to be disclosed before the assessment can be made. Sometimes issues of confidentiality prevent this from happening, although for Balanced Scorecard projects this is not usually the case.

We have used this approach to predict the success and failure of Balanced Scorecard projects in a number of organisations and it is effective in identifying success and failure. However, it does have one blind spot. Many Balanced Scorecard initiatives fail through interference from the parent organisation. These interventions are not always foreseen by the local management, and therefore are not picked up with this approach, unless the interviews are extended to the parent organisation itself.

Summary of pre-assessment

Here we have looked at three specific tools for analysing change.

- Force-field analysis is a quick and easily used tool to assess subjectively the main forces advancing and impeding the change.
- Change responses is a tool which categorises individuals into four groups to identify allies, enemies and those simply sitting on the fence.
- Priority, effort and reward assessment looks at change from the perspective of different projects competing for management attention.

Before a major change initiative begins, it is well worth conducting some form of assessment and these three tools should help you to do this. However, they are also useful as the project progresses. Why has your Balanced Scorecard initiative stalled? Is it resistance, or is the organisation simply overloaded with what it is trying to achieve?

So now let us move onto the process of implementation itself.

How do you successfully implement a Balanced Scorecard?

In Chapter 1 we described the 'opening questions' you needed to ask before undertaking the project. Let us expand on these, beginning with the 4Ps.

Before starting

Ken Platts came up with the idea of 4Ps, the factors you need to consider before you embark on a project such as a Balanced Scorecard Implementation. They are:

1. **Point of entry:** obtaining the understanding and commitment of the management group, clearly defining expectations;
2. **Participation:** individual and group participation to achieve enthusiasm, understanding and commitment; workshop-style meetings to agree objectives, identify problems, develop improvement and catalyse involvement; a decision making forum;
3. **Project management:** adequate resources and an agreed timescale;
4. **Procedure:** well-defined with stages of information gathering, information analysis and identifying improvements using simple tools and techniques including a written record of the result of each stage.

Let us just expand a little on each of these.

Point of entry

This is concerned with how you launch such an initiative. Getting buy in from the senior management team is important, as are managing expectations and setting the rules of the game. The approach we usually take is to emphasise the learning approach that will be adopted. How we will examine the current business objectives and develop new goals from an analysis of the owners, customers and other stakeholder requirements. It is also useful here to consider how the project is to be launched to the rest of the organisation. Is the initial work going to be done without an explicit announcement and the Balanced Scorecard presented at a time when the project is already well under way, or is there a big announcement and the work then follows? Both approaches can be appropriate depending on the organisation's circumstances and history with such initiatives.

Participation

Who do you involve and who do you leave out? You will need to involve the team of managers or directors running the organisation for which you are developing the scorecard. This will take quite a chunk of their time, but it is worth their effort to take part. During the workshops you are creating dissatisfaction with the current situation and presenting a vision of the future; you are also outlining the first steps of the implementation. If individuals are missing, then only part of the team has bought into the process.

Each team member will have a different perspective on the organisation and the issues and priorities facing it. For example, the sales director may see one customer as being highly valued because of the volume of orders placed. The same customer could be seen as a real problem in manufacturing because of the disruption his orders cause due to last minute changes of specification, whilst the finance director may be concerned about the customer's ability to pay. This is a simple example, but the different perspectives are important and build a better picture of the current situation and future issues.

Finally, there may be an issue with the person who is being left out. In one organisation, the engineering director was not involved. It became obvious very quickly that the rest of the board had an issue with how engineering was performing, but trying to run the process without the engineering director present only exacerbated the issue.

Project management

Any initiative on the scale of a Balanced Scorecard implementation requires project managing from the start. The initial workshops require support and co-ordination is needed between the workshops to ensure that actions are taken and that all those involved are ready for the next stage. Obviously, once all the objectives and measures have been agreed and approved, there is a significant role to play in getting them implemented and having a project manager involved from the start is critical.

Procedure

The workshops and exercises undertaken by the team form the procedure. For this to be effective you need to spell out clearly the stages the team will work through to develop the scorecard. The objective is to break the task down into manageable chunks and to guide the discussion so that topics are debated logically in sequence.

The tools help structure the conversation and stop participants deviating from the subject. The idea is to allow discussion and even argument, but once a position has been agreed, it should be recorded and the debate should move to the next topic.

The change formula

The change formula was proposed Mr Gleicher of Arthur D Little in the 1960s (Buchanan and Huczynski, 1997, p. 473). His suggestion was that change only occurs when three things are present as captured here.

$$K \times D \times V > C$$

when   K represents **K**nowledge of first practical steps
         D represents **D**issatisfaction with the status quo
         V represents the desirability of the **V**ision of the future
         C represents the **C**ost, both material and psychological, of doing something

Gleicher argued that you needed to be dissatisfied with the current situation, have a vision of a better way of doing things and a knowledge of the first steps to get there. These are multiplied together and the product has to be greater than the cost of making the change. The multiplication is very important, because as Gleicher argued, if any one element is missing (i.e. it is equal to zero) then the whole of the left-hand side of the equation becomes zero and change does not occur.

The process approach described in this book is designed to support the scorecard implementation by addressing the three aspects of Gleicher's equation. To put it simply, the assessment of the stakeholder needs (described in Chapter 3) creates the dissatisfaction with what we is happening at present. The creation of the success map develops a vision of the future and the tools and techniques we are describing (Chapters 4, 5, 6 and 7) create the knowledge of the first steps taken to move the scorecard forward.

One point is worth stressing: the equation talks about a 'knowledge of the first steps'. The emphasis is on 'first'. The process approach described here is a learning process. It is designed to engage the whole team in a debate about what is important for the organisation and its future. If those trying to implement the system appear to have all the answers themselves before the process starts, then other people just think they are being 'taken for a ride'. On the other hand, if the general direction is not mapped out and the steps defined, people may feel rudderless. There is a delicate balance between these two situations.

To achieve this you need to define the process steps in advance, so that everyone knows what they are discussing, at which stage and why. However, the outcome of those discussions has to be left to the workshops themselves.

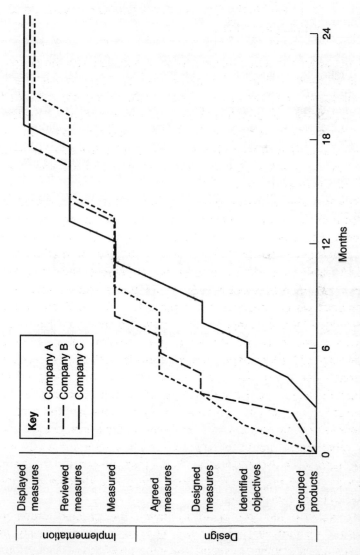

Figure 5.4: Chart of performance measurement systems development

How long does it take?

Figure 5.4 shows the graph of Balanced Scorecard implementations in three different companies. As you will see from the graph, the implementation can take some considerable time; exactly how long will depend on the size and complexity of the organisation.

It takes several weeks to work through the workshops needed to create your Balanced Scorecard. However, it can then take between 9 and 13 months until the scorecard reaches the stage where the measures are on display around the organisation.

Why is this? Apart from the time required to produce and implement the measures, it takes time for the management to become comfortable with the data and for them to allow for it to be displayed. Fortunately, when the scorecard is updated, the process moves more swiftly.

Why do Balanced Scorecard implementations fail?

There are three reasons why Balanced Scorecard implementations fail:

1. senior management support is lacking or wanes over the course of the project
2. parent company interventions
3. fear of measurement.

There are also two hurdles – excuses for why some companies succeed and others fail. They are called 'hurdles' because all companies face these two issues, but some companies jump over them and others do not. These hurdles are:

1. lack of time and effort available
2. issues with IT systems.

We will address these each in turn, starting with the three showstoppers and then finishing with the two hurdles.

Senior management support

Senior management support is cited as critical in all the literature on implementation and change. However, what is not often noted is that this support has to be maintained throughout the project and is dynamic.

From your initial pre-assessments you should have developed a good understanding of the level of support you have. You then need to maintain that support throughout the project.

So how can you create and maintain senior management support? We suggest the following plan:

1. Create a coalition of people who are committed to the scorecard at the outset and launch the project in a positive way with this group's support.
2. Engage the whole of the management team in the process of building the scorecard. This will require them to attend the workshops and work through the development of the success map and the measures.
3. Plan and support the process with some project co-ordination and management so the workshops are productive.
4. Facilitate the workshops so the tools are explained and used effectively.
5. Ensure that genuine concerns and legitimate contrary points of view are raised and discussed in the workshops.
6. Ensure the workshops are the forums in which the real discussions take place and the real decisions are made. If people believe they can then alter decisions after the workshops, the process will break down. However, if a

valid concern has been raised afterwards, bring it back for formal discussion at the next workshop to preserve the integrity of the process.

7. Reach a consensus at each stage before moving forward to the next.
8. Record the outcomes as they are agreed.
9. Ensure agreed actions are taken.

Typically, the more heated the debate, the better (provided you can bring it to consensus at the end). The strength of debate will confirm that all parties are taking the process seriously. The debate will ensure opposing views are heard and discussed at length and will usually create new insights into the priorities for the business. The insight creates and reinforces senior management commitment to continue with the project and implement the measures.

Parent company intervention

Parent company actions are amongst the greatest source of Balanced Scorecard failures. In our experience, two-thirds of the failures occur as a direct result of changes introduced by the parent organisations. This is not usually deliberate, but the results are still the same. Here are some examples:

1. Restructuring, merging divisions, changing the focus of business units and closing operations will have a direct impact. The result is that you either have a Balanced Scorecard designed for an organisation that does not exist any more or you have a Balanced Scorecard that no longer reflects the new direction of the business.
2. Parent company initiatives: many groups embark on global initiatives which then receive top management attention, time and resources. Key projects to watch out for are benchmarking projects and quality awards (EFQM,

Baldridge, etc.) as these take a slightly different approach to performance measurement. If they are not carefully handled, you will find the emphasis going elsewhere and the scorecard project stalled at the very least.

3. Resourcing: you need some slack resource to undertake this kind of initiative. If key team players are seconded to other projects, this slack resource is soon consumed. If the team leader is lost or promoted, this can have a devastating impact.

Real failures

A central European manufacturing plant We had reached the stage of agreeing all the measures when the parent company announced a world wide competitive benchmarking project across all it sites. 'This is what the rewards and stars were being given for' said the local general manager. So they abandoned the scorecard and focused on what head office wanted.

A metals business We developed a Balanced Scorecard for three main divisions in the same group of companies. It emerged that in parallel, senior management was reviewing the organisation's structure resulting in the merger of three divisions. We were therefore left with a scorecard designed for divisions that no longer existed and we had to start again with the new business structure.

> **A high tech company** This company was going through a period of considerable capital investment and growth. Senior management was stretched, but decided to progress the scorecard project. Half way through this project, the parent company decided to remove half the local management team. The project stopped immediately.

How do you deal with this problem? Our suggestion would be to approach the level of management above and explain the situation and get their buy-in to the scorecard project before you start. Your management team may or may not want to do this, but the question you need to ask is 'does the management team have the discretion to launch and complete a scorecard project without the consent of the parent organisation?'

Fear of measurement

In some situations Balanced Scorecard projects can fail owing to a fear of measurement. The most usual situation is where those being measured fear the retribution of their managers. There is a second less frequent situation that occurs when the managers themselves do not want to publicise the results of measurement.

> **How bad can it be?** In a rare case, a divisional management team was instructed to undertake a Balanced Scorecard project by their divisional managing director. On completion, there was a real resistance to implementing the measures. After a series of board meetings where various excuses were made, the managing director announced that any director who had not completed their measures by the next meeting would be sacked. At the next meeting all the directors turned

up, no one had done their measures and the project was rapidly forgotten. It emerged afterwards that the directors were more worried about the measures than they were about losing their jobs. The company had an extreme blame culture and the senior team was not prepared to give the managing director any more tools to chastise them with.

Lifting the stone   Have you ever lifted a stone and seen all the bugs crawling around underneath it? Well that was the way a Balanced Scorecard project was described to me by one director. He had spent all the time and effort creating a scorecard and had engaged his team in the project. But when 'push came to shove' he didn't implement it because he believed that the project would expose him to too many questions.

'When I go to board meetings, I am the director with the biggest order book and making the most profit' he said. 'Do I want to use the scorecard to expose that I have to longest list of overdue orders, or the highest levels of work in progress? No I don't.'

Changing the company culture to overcome this problem is not easy. If you think your company fits into this category, you should think very carefully about whether the scorecard project is the best project to progress at this time.

What are the hurdles to be overcome?

So finally we come to the problem of hurdles that we outlined above. Lack of time and effort available and issues with IT systems are always cited as reasons why scorecard implementations have failed. The interesting fact, however, is that nearly all organisations run into these problems. Successful organisations overcome the hurdles and others do not.

Our message is to expect time and effort and the IT system to be an issue. Try to plan the project in a way that releases resources to help it succeed and to reduce the number of other competing initiatives that are being undertaken at the same time. Expect and plan the need for IT resource to support the project and manage expectations so that people do not expect the measures to appear as if by magic the day after they have agreed them.

But it is continued support, persistence and top management commitment that will see you over these hurdles.

Conclusion

When implementing a Balanced Scorecard you need to remember the following:

This is a long march

Changes can be categorised into bold strokes and long marches. The implementation of a Balanced Scorecard is a long march. It takes time to design and develop the measures, it takes time to embed them in the organisation and to get them accepted. So prepare for this and manage expectations from the outset.

You must have strategic discretion

Given the majority of initiatives fail as a direct result of interference from the parent company, you must ensure you have the strategic discretion to undertake such a project. If there is any doubt, discuss this with those concerned in advance and gain their understanding and commitment.

You need serious top management support

You cannot take this support for granted and you need it throughout the process. You have to manage it as it will ebb and flow over time.

You must not be overloaded with initiatives

Most companies are trying to do more projects than they have the capacity to deliver. You should be aware of other initiatives that take executive time. But also think about the timing of the initiative. Is it a busy time of year? Should it be done before the budgeting round? These are all questions that can help you guide the project through the trials of implementation.

You need a receptive culture

As we saw, a blame culture will seriously impede the implementation of a Balanced Scorecard. However, the process approach we have suggested can significantly change this culture, especially if the management style is directed to focusing on the systemic causes of under performance rather than focusing on who is to blame.

You need a good process

We have described this in the preceding chapters.

You need to build commitment during the process

The quality of the debate during the process has a great impact on the commitment to implement. This commitment will carry you across the implementation 'valley of death'. Be ready for the valley of death. After the initial euphoria of agreeing the new measures there will be a period when the data has to be collected, the systems set up and the measures reported. It is a difficult period when patience and persistence is required. You will need to manage expectations here too.

Integrate everything you have done

Try to build on the past and not throw out old initiatives. Most organisations have a habit of wanting to start from a clean sheet of paper. This has its benefits, but often previous initiatives are abandoned and managers become very cynical about whether they should bother to engage with new change projects as these are inevitably swept away with the next round of changes. Some of the best Balanced Scorecard implementations have built on past projects. One company was doing TQM, and called the Balanced Scorecard initiative, 'TQM with bite'. As a result, we built on all the TQM work that had gone before, aligning this with the new measures. Twelve months later, we did this again, as the appraisal system needed updating. We aligned the appraisal objectives with the Balanced Scorecard measures.

In this chapter we have focused on how to implement the Balanced Scorecard. In the next chapter, we will look at how you use the scorecard to manage the business.

INSTANT TIP

There is a process for designing and implementing a Balanced Scorecard. It requires senior line managers to be involved.

06

How do you manage through measurement?

Introduction

The previous chapters have focused on how to design and implement a Balanced Scorecard. In this chapter we will talk about how you use the measures to manage your business. The Balanced Scorecard and success maps are effective ways of establishing your position, communicating direction and starting to align activity with strategy. But to manage through measures you really need to stimulate the right actions, influence behaviour and learn from measurement.

To do this we will talk about two different types of review. The first is the performance review of individual measures; the second is the performance review of an organisation.

Performance reviews are probably the most overlooked subject in performance measurement. Some companies do them well, but few companies have a structured approach that they apply consistently across the business. So we will start by explaining why this step is so important.

Why is managing through measures so important?

There are many benefits from designing a performance measurement system. People learn to understand the business better, they create an agreed success map and the process helps establish priorities. But until the measures are used to take action, the whole approach does not take root in the organisation. If it does not take root, the measurement system will quickly fall into disuse and all the hard work establishing the Balanced Scorecard in the first place will be forgotten.

We never believe a Balanced Scorecard has been implemented until the performance measures are publicly on display around the organisation. This may be on the notice boards in the various departments or the canteen. Alternatively, it may be on an intranet with universal accessibility. In either case, the measures are there for the entire organisation to see. They give good news as well as bad. They are visible and everyone in the organisation knows when they haven't been updated and the reporting is out of date.

Making the scorecard visible is the first step in communicating your business objectives to the whole organisation. But you will still have to act on the measures if you are going to change performance. Managing the review process is essential in ensuring measures are used.

How do you ensure measures are used?

There are two sides to this:

- creating a culture in which your measures are perceived as being important for the business;

- reviewing individual measures, concentrating effort on making changes which will have the most positive impact on your performance.

The following examples show how you can make sure your measures are used.

Asking questions A colleague of ours had developed a measurement system for a drinks company. It had been installed and all the measures were available on the intranet, but the managing director, who was located at head office in London, was concerned because he felt the system was not being used properly. Our colleague's solution was to encourage the managing director to open the measurement system every morning when he arrived at work and then ring the plant manager, asking for an explanation of the previous day's performance. It only took a few days for the plant manager to be asking his staff the questions in preparation for the MD's phone call, and the whole system suddenly became the centre of conversation.

Debate not blame After implementing a measurement system in the UK subsidiary of an international drugs company, the managing director was extremely keen to ensure that the system was kept up to date and used by all his staff. As a result, he built an intranet with all the performance measures displayed, along with the success map and supporting information including the definitions of the measures held in the record sheet format. Everyone in the organisation had access to all the data with the exception of the profitability figures that were kept confidential (because the parent company was listed). However, financial performance was reported as percentage of budget achieved. The system rapidly highlighted where data was missing, so the MD could chase up anyone who was not keeping the system up to date. He could also drill down into the system to understand where the business was performing well and where it was not. However, the MD was very careful in the way he used the system to avoid it being seen as a big stick for driving the company. When he did identify things that were going wrong, he used the measures and the system to have a debate about what was happening and what could be done to rectify the situation, rather than for blaming those involved for poor performance. During its first three months of operation, the use of the system grew rapidly until over two thirds of all staff were using it to access performance data.

The importance of measures Mike's former boss, Glyn, used to have performance information given to him, or telephoned to his home, at the end of every shift. The operation ran 24 hours a day for seven days a week and included a summary of the night shift at 7.30 every Saturday and Sunday morning. Giving Glyn the figures in this way emphasised the importance of the shift's performance. It communicated how important the figures were in a way that is never communicated in a report.

How do you review the performance of a single measure?

The examples above show how you can begin to create a culture in which performance measures are seen as being vital to the organisation. However, in addition, you need a robust review process. In the following section we describe two tools which will help you to do this.

The performance measure control sheet will help you to focus on the most important outcomes from each measure. The performance planning value chain will help you in structuring the review process itself.

We will start by explaining how to review individual measures and by introducing the performance measure control sheet.

The performance measure control sheet

There are five actions that are essential for managing performance using measures.

1. Understand what the measure is telling you about the activity it is measuring.
2. Analyse the underlying causes of the variation in performance.
3. Plan your action.
4. Ensure the action is taken.
5. Study the impact the action has on performance.

But before we show you a tool for bringing these five elements together, we will talk about natural variation and management interventions. If you are to manage with measures effectively, you need to understand the concept of normal variation and when to take action on the measures.

Performance variation

How do you assess performance? In the UK many of us listen to Radio 4 in the morning when the hot topics of the day are discussed. It is usual to hear a debate about a set of figures where politicians are arguing whether a situation is getting better or worse. They do this by comparing the latest figure to last year's or the latest figure against what it was under the last government. They are choosing their figures carefully in order to support their point. However, there is a fundamental flaw in this process. What they are doing is comparing two random numbers. Ideally, what you need to do is to compare the aggregate levels of performance over time. To do this you need time series data (data presented on a graph, plotted over time).

There is usually a problem with time series data in that it is not a straight line. If you measure anything over time the line fluctuates up and down. This is natural variation. In fact if there is no natural variation you should be concerned.

Beware of flat lines   To a doctor a flat line usually means the patient is dead. This is also true in business as there is natural variation in everything we do. The night shift of a foundry in the north of England had a very consistent output. For many weeks it achieved a perfect standard output. Early one morning the production manager was leaving to visit a customer and as he drove over the hill he could see the foundry and the smokeless chimney. He was immediately concerned that they had had a breakdown, so he made a detour. When he arrived at the foundry he discovered the night shift were asleep. His subsequent investigations revealed that for many weeks the night shift production had been made on the day shift and an ingenious scheme had been set up to book the output to the night shift.

Let us take a simple example of variation from everyday life. How long does it take you to travel to work in the morning? Your answer will probably be: 'It depends.' So what does it depend on? Pippa drives to work. On a good day the traffic on the A14 may be light; the traffic lights are green and she arrives at the Institute's office a few minutes quicker than normal. But some days, things seem to conspire against her and it takes a little longer. So, if she measures her journey time, it fluctuates a few minutes each day. When she gets up in the morning, does she know if it is going to be a good journey or not? Not really. It is difficult to predict. If it is raining, she will know the odds are against her, but even on a sunny day, a tractor may slow her down. All she can do is predict the journey time within a limit of plus or minus five minutes. So what time does she leave for work? If she wants to be on time, she needs to allow for the average journey time plus five minutes. If she does not allow the extra five minutes then she will arrive late on 50 per cent of the days.

But occasionally something really goes wrong. It snows and the journey takes four hours. If there is an accident and the road is closed, the diversion can easily take an additional 30 minutes. So how does she react to these events? If she is 30 minutes late because of an accident, does she always leave 30 minutes early or does she leave four hours early because of the outside possibility of heavy snow? The answer is no. She understands these are special situations and acts accordingly.

What we are illustrating here is the difference between normal variation in the journey time to work and the exceptions. If Pippa considers a normal journey and tries to analyse why she was a few minutes early or late, there is usually a set of random causes. There is a build-up of traffic in one place and a clear run in another. On the other hand, on the days when Pippa is significantly delayed, there is usually one single and obvious cause. Therefore, we need to distinguish between normal variation and special causes.

One of the first steps you need to take when analysing performance is to understand the difference between normal variation and special causes. In fact, we can define normal variation as the natural variation in performance for which it is 'not economic' to identify the cause. On the other hand, special causes can be easily and cheaply identified and acted upon.

Normal variation – special causes   In making PVCu windows the frames, transoms and mullions are welded together by heating up the plastic and pressing the pieces firmly together until they fuse. The strength of the resulting joints is important for the integrity of the window, so it was measured regularly. There were always slight variations. Plate temperature, the age of the teflon coating and the temperature of the material all caused small variations in the process. However, occasionally there was a major reduction in strength. Analysis pointed to a problem around 9.30–10.30 in the morning, but only on some days. The tea break was one possible explanation – but that happened every day. The plant manager eventually realised that deliveries often occurred at that time and the welder was near the big door. A strong, cold draught was a special cause.

Astronomical causes?   One company nearly called in an astrologer to help with their performance problems. Making detergents for many years, they were concerned about having poor quality batches on a monthly basis. A new production manager wanted to make his mark so he attacked this issue –

but no cause could be found. Extensive detailed analysis showed that the cycle was not actually the true calendar month but followed a lunar cycle – hence the call for an astrologer. The real cause was high tides and salt water ingress into parts of the process. An astronomical special cause!

How do you identify special causes?

During your drive to work you can identify special causes as they occur, but if you are not that close to the process, it may be more difficult. One way you can do this is through statistical process control charts (SPC charts).

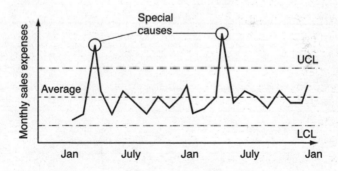

Figure 6.1: The sales expenses control chart

When you construct an SPC chart you use the variation in the data to calculate the limits of normal variation. These are called the 'upper' and 'lower' control limits. When an observation falls outside these limits, it is invariably a special cause.

By plotting your measures over time on a chart with the upper and lower control limit clearly shown, you can identify the normal variation and special causes. Take the example in Figure 6.1. This is the graph of a sales team's travel expenses over a two-year period. It goes up and down over the years but there is a month in both years when the expenditure is unusually high. It is not in the same month each year so it is not an annual cycle. However, the real cause of this special expenditure was the annual sales conference, held at the end of March one year and the beginning of April in the next.

Creating an SPC chart Software is now available to do this for you. If you have a significant amount of data or want to do a detailed analysis, this is the route to take. However, we will show the calculations in a simple exercise below, which shows a table of number of late trains each month.

Month	Number of late trains	Variance
Jan	19	
Feb	21	2
Mar	18	3
Apr	15	3
May	15	0
June	22	7
July	30	8
Aug	25	5
Sept	19	6
Oct	17	2
Total	201	36
Mean	20.1	4

1. Calculate the mean from the number of late trains you have observed. In this case it is 201 / 10 = 20.1.
2. Calculate the variation between each of the two results, this should be an absolute variation, so all the results are positive.
3. Calculate the mean of the variation. In this case it is 36 / 9 = 4.
4. Multiply the mean of the variation by 2.66. (2.66 is the constant used to calculate control limits – or for statisticians – the 3 sigma limit). In this case 4 × 2.66 = 10.64.
5. Calculate the upper control limit by adding the 10.64 to the average, giving 30.74.
6. Calculate the lower control limit by subtracting 10.64 from the average, giving 9.46.

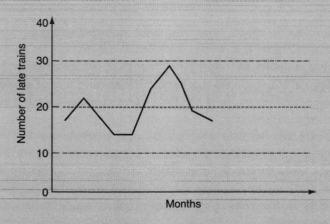

Figure 6.2: A statistical process control chart

In the example above, you can now see quite clearly that there were no special causes in the ten months of the report. So how many late trains would you expect in November and December? Given the chart above, it would be reasonable to expect between 9 and 31. That is assuming the way you run the network remains the same and that there is no special cause, namely heavy snow.

To summarise: special causes are those that are economically worthwhile identifying and separating for management action. You can identify these through statistical techniques and the points lying outside your control limits are those you should investigate first.

When should you take action?

The reason we are discussing normal variation and special causes is because they need to be managed differently. If you treat normal variation as a special cause, you will actually make performance worse.

Tampering is often observed with quarterly targets and bonuses (see Figure 6.3). Here, the sales in the first month of the quarter are reduced as sales have been brought forward to the previous quarter to achieve the target. The second month's sales are usually quite normal but the third month peaks, creating the classic saw tooth pattern.

The problem is that the sales team's response to the performance target creates a series of surges in demand for the operations department to cope with. To satisfy demand, the company will have to resource for the higher levels of throughput which occur every three months. Doing this is wasteful and will reduce profitability.

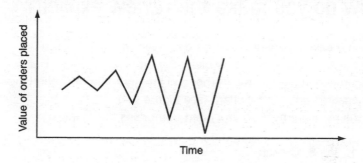

Figure 6.3: The impact of quarterly sales bonus

So, the message is: do not react to normal variation by focusing on each data point. Variation is reduced and performance is improved by focusing instead on the process. However, when you observe a special cause – one that falls outside your control limits – you should investigate and remove the source if necessary.

The steps you should take in managing the performance of a specific measure are as follows:

1. Collect and plot the data over time.
2. Once you have collected a reasonable set of data points (8–10), calculate the average and the upper and lower control limits.
3. Identify the data points that fall outside these control limits (the special causes).
4. Address these special causes and take steps to eliminate them from the process.
5. Once the special causes have been addressed, concentrate on all the factors that come together to cause the rest of the natural variation.
6. Once you have reduced the variation, focus on improving the process as a whole.

How do you make the review explicit?

In some cases measures will be displayed in the form of an SPC chart with annotation to explain the special causes. But we recommend you go a step further and integrate the SPC chart into a 'measurement control chart' (see Figure 6.4).

The measurement control chart comprises four panels:

1. the SPC chart
2. the analysis sheet
3. the action planning chart
4. the implementation control chart.

The measurement control chart enables you to work through a cycle of observing what is happening, analysing the causes, planning action and monitoring its implementation. The last panel then allows you to study the impact on performance in the next period. Over time, a picture will develop of what has happened, what has worked and what has not.

The following are examples of charts from a process manufacturing plant.

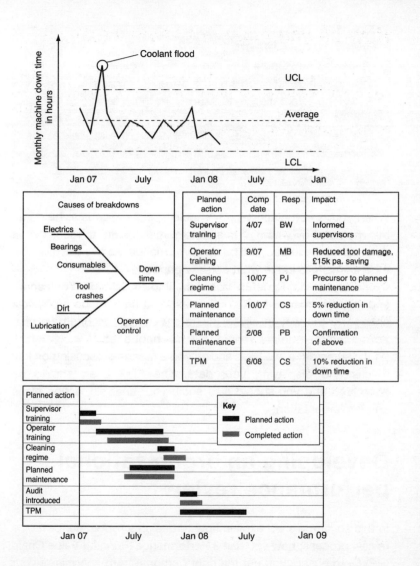

Figure 6.4: The performance measure control chart

Practical problems

When you implement this in your own organisation, you will find your biggest problem will be ensuring the analysis is done. The temptation is to jump from the measure to action without investigating the root causes. It can take time to establish the root causes and it is necessary to look at the information in a number of different ways to find out what is happening. Some people are not comfortable doing that.

When you plan the action, you should specify what is to be done, by when and by whom. It is also extremely useful to record what you expect the impact will be on performance, as this will give you a benchmark to judge what actually happens.

Finally, do not forget to record the implementation. You cannot expect performance to change unless you have made a physical change to the way in which things are done. Too often we plan action and then do not verify that it has happened.

To summarise, we have shown you a means of focusing on key results and displaying your data. The SPC chart should be annotated and you should also show your analysis, action plans and implementation.

Developing an organisational performance review

In this section we will explain how to design a robust performance review process; how you use a Performance Planning Value Chain (PPVC) to ensure you get the right outcome from analysis of your data and finally we will give an example of the structure for a performance review meeting.

The performance planning value chain is a simple framework developed by the Centre for Business Performance at Cranfield School of Management to help define the process required to conduct a good performance measurement review.

It is a simple framework that outlines the seven steps you need to take in extracting value from your data (see Figure 6.5).

The seven steps are:

1. Developing a question.
2. Gathering the data.
3. Analysing the data.
4. Interpreting the data.
5. Engaging the decision-makers.
6. Making the decision.
7. Taking action.

We describe these in more detail below.

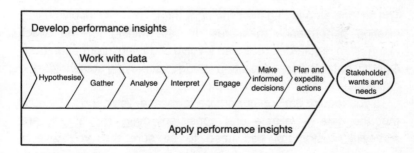

Figure 6.5: The performance planning value chain developed by the Centre for Business Performance

Developing the question

The start of the process is developing a question to be answered or developing a hypothesis to be tested.

A question might be:

'How do our customers perceive our current service levels?'

Alternatively, a hypothesis might be:

'Investment in a new customer relations management system will increase customer satisfaction. Is this actually happening?'

Posing a question gives focus to performance measurement and is an important first step in extracting value from data. It guides all the subsequent steps.

Gathering data

The second step is to gather the right data. This may involve using existing performance measures or data mining for the exact information required. It may also involve acquiring information from external data sources, and often includes surveying stakeholders – customers, consumers and employees.

If you require data on current performance, you need to be sure that the data is reliable and consistent over time. If you are surveying customers, you need to be sure that you take a representative sample of sufficient size so you can be confident in the results after data analysis. In many organisations, clean data is not always available, although if you have designed and implemented the performance measures correctly, you will have made a good start. If the data is not clean, you may still be able to use it, but it needs to be treated very carefully and those making decisions need to be aware of the potential shortcomings.

Analysing data

Whatever the context, some form of data analysis needs to be undertaken. Far too often, organisations act on management intuition or anecdotes without taking into account what the data is telling them. Intuition has its place, but it is all the better for being informed by analysis of the data.

Having gathered the right data, it needs to be analysed methodically. There is a need to understand what the current level of performance is, the underlying trend in performance and what factors have an impact on the level of performance being achieved.

Statistical process control is one useful technique for identifying the level of performance and the trend over time. When used by those directly involved in the organisation and the processes, the technique can help determine root causes of the major influences on performance.

Interpreting data

Data analysis is not enough. It needs to be interpreted. This is done by putting the data into a context that gives the information meaning.

To give an example. If you conduct a customer satisfaction survey and get a result of '4' (customers satisfied), what does that mean? You need the context to interpret the result.

There are obvious comparisons you can make. How does this compare with the last survey? How does this compare with your competitors' survey results? How does this compare with the rest of your industry or with other industries? This contextual information gives meaning to the result and enables you to interpret the data.

Engaging the decision-makers

Having interpreted the data, it is then important to communicate, especially to those who need to take action. This may involve presenting the data graphically in a way that grabs people's attention. It may involve creating a story that resonates with people in the business and sticks in their minds. It has been reported that:

● Jan Timmer, when he was CEO of Philips, went as far as issuing a hypothetical press release to his top team announcing the bankruptcy of the corporation to get their full attention;

● at AstraZenica they have been in the habit of conducting performance reviews by looking for stories from around the organisation which highlight particular aspects of performance or dilemmas the company faces.

In the Centre for Business Performance we found that people didn't fully engage with our own performance reports. The solution was to produce a front page similar to the headlines of a newspaper.

Making the decision

Sometimes, when all the work with the data has been completed, the decision is obvious.

When he was Chairman of British Leyland, Lord Stokes once said that by the time a decision climbed the organisation to reach him, the difference between the options was so fine that his decision would make little difference to the business outcome.

Sometimes, a decision just has to be made, but you shouldn't just be tossing a coin. The decision should fit with the company's values and culture; it should be implementable and support other strategic initiatives. This requires judgement and that, of course, is where senior executives earn their money.

Taking action

Decisions are only valuable if they are acted upon. It is very easy to produce a list of actions; the problem is usually that they are not completed. It is important to prioritise and pick the few most important actions and then make sure they happen.

Creating value

The outcome of the previous steps should add value to the company by satisfying the requirements of the various stakeholders. Too often we do not check whether the actions we take actually create value. To do this we should close the loop by developing a new hypothesis to test.

The PPVC has been described as a sequential process. In practice you will find the outcomes at certain stages will mean you have to return to the beginning and rework earlier stages in the light of your findings. The PPVC provides a checklist of all the stages you need to take on order to have confidence in what the data is telling you.

How should you structure a performance review meeting?

To review the overall performance of the organisation, you should set up a review meeting with appropriate managers and draw up a structured agenda. You will need to decide how much preparation is undertaken before the performance review meeting. The PPVC is important because you want to be certain that the data and information you are presenting to the review is correct. There is a balance to be struck between presenting raw data which may be meaningless, and a fait accompli which may be rejected. The panel should be involved in the interpretation, and creation of insight, so they engage with the information provided and they are comfortable with the actions they agree.

The following approach has been used successfully in DHL both to manage the UK business (Neely et al., 2002) and to manage their international security operation. In this way you will focus on answering the key questions about the organisation's performance, rather than focusing only on whether targets were met.

1. Agree in advance the agenda for the review meeting. We have shown an example of an agenda taken from a training business below.
2. Have the data from the measures and other sources prepared before the meeting. The information prepared for presentation should answer the questions on the agenda.
3. At the review meeting, consider each perspective of the Balanced Scorecard in turn. Ideally, an analyst (not the person responsible for the performance) should present the data. This makes the review less personal and allows the responsible manager to participate in the discussion without becoming defensive.
4. At the end of each perspective, list the actions that have been discussed and then move onto the next perspective.
5. Once all the perspectives have been reviewed, the action list should be reviewed. Most companies try to implement too many actions. So the list should be prioritised and a realistic action list agreed.
6. Finally, review the meeting format to ensure everything has gone as well as it possibly could, or to capture the learning points for structuring the next meeting.

Training business performance review agenda This company runs open courses designed for individual business people and tailor made training programmes which are run in-company.

Employee and development perspective
Have our actions from the last meeting been completed?

How happy are our associate lecturers?

- Are we keeping them busy and retaining their loyalty?
- Do we have sufficient contact with them?
- Do we have any feedback from them?

How are our staff?

- Are there any specific issues?
- Are we retaining the people we want?
- What is the level of absenteeism? Is it acceptable?
- What are the development activities, courses attended?
- Have we arranged any benchmarking visits?

How healthy is our course programme?

- Do we have sufficient new proposals?
- Are we launching new events?
- Do we need to revise or remove any courses?
- Are there any specific quality issues?

What are the actions following this review?

Operational perspective

Have our actions from the last meeting been completed?

How effective is our administration?

- Are course handouts of good quality?
- Are handouts produced on time?
- Is material up to date?
- Have delegates raised any issues about the venue?

How effective is our marketing operation?

- Do we have enough contacts on our marketing database?
- Are we sure we are marketing to active contacts?
- What is the level of mailing returns? Is this acceptable?
- What is the number of email responses returned, opened, click throughs?
- How many hits are there on our website? What are the most popular pages?
- What are the campaign booking rates? How do they compare with past experience?
- How are people booking – web, phone, mailed booking forms?

How effective are our in-company programmes?

- What are the enquiry rates?
- How many companies have our development managers visited?
- What are our tender success rates?
- What are the reasons for tender failure?

What are the actions following this review?

Customer perspective
Have our actions from the last meeting been completed?
How satisfied are our customers?

- How have delegates rated our courses?
- Are there any specific comments we need to note?
- Feedback from key account visits?
- What is the level of repeat bookings? How does this compare with the equivalent period last year?

What are the actions following this review?

Financial perspective
Have our actions from the last meeting been completed?
How profitable is our open programme?

- Numbers per course day?
- Numbers against forecast?
- Contribution per course?

How profitable is our in-company training business?

- Income per course day?
- Income per business development manager?
- Contribution against budget?

How profitable is the business?

- Income per employee?

- Income per programme day?
- Venue utilisation?
- Forward bookings and committed business?
- Income and expenditure against budget?

What are the actions following this review?

Summary
Prioritise and agree specific actions to be taken
Review the meeting

- Are we asking the right questions?
- Are we receiving the right information?
- Any other issues of concern?

An agenda such as this allows you to blend quantitative data from your measures with qualitative feedback, enriching your decision-making process.

There is one final point to note here. You should consider how often you need to run your review meetings. DHL used to have a monthly meeting, but found when they operated in this way, they did not have time to implement the actions and see the impact of these actions on performance before they had the next meeting. For them, a quarterly meeting was more appropriate. You may need a monthly meeting to report results to your parent organisation, but many organisations are better managed through quarterly performance reviews.

Conclusion

In this chapter we have focused on how you can translate performance measurement into performance management. We have shown you a framework for reviewing individual measures and introduced you to a way of conducting organisational level performance reviews.

For the Balanced Scorecard to deliver value, the measures need to be cascaded down the organisation. But as performance improvement only comes from taking action, it is also important to cascade the review process. In our experience, most employees do not understand the goals and objectives of the business. Cascading the measures and the review process is an effect way of ensuring the objectives are widely communicated and that you stimulate action and learning from the use of the measures.

INSTANT TIP

The best way to manage performance is to ask the important questions and use the measures to answer them.

07

How do you keep your scorecard up to date?

Introduction

The Balanced Scorecard must always be kept up to date so it reflects the current situation and the competitive imperatives. If this doesn't happen, it rapidly loses its credibility and legitimacy. Worse still, it means that new strategies are held back by the old performance measures.

In this chapter, we will describe the different reviews that are needed to keep the Balanced Scorecard up to date. We will give examples of how this can be done and we will highlight the barriers that get in the way.

We don't have a strategy! I went down to the West of England to talk to a managing director about designing and implementing a performance measurement system. After a long debate about what he thought the benefits of the measurement system would be for the company and what the issues might be, the MD stopped the discussion and said:

'Before we go any further, I would like you to do two things. I would like you to go round our factory and see what we do and I would like you to meet my senior team.'

I had no objection to either, and was escorted to the next room by the MD's secretary. Here, all the senior managers sat around a central island with adjoining desks. I was introduced to the head of HR.

'Why are you here?', she asked.
'I have come to talk about implementing a new performance measurement system.'
'Great idea', she replied, 'It's just a pity we don't have a strategy.'

That is a common response from people in many companies, so I didn't pay a great deal of attention to the remark, but as I walked round the central desk, six out of the eight senior managers present made a similar comment.

I left on the tour of the factory wondering how I was going to tell the managing director that six of his eight direct reports didn't think the company had a strategy.

The factory visit was an eye opener. The factory was beautifully run. There was evidence of TPM (Total Preventative Maintenance) and brand-new equipment, which had just arrived from the manufacturers, was sitting on the side as the company had found faults before it was installed.

Half an hour later, I was back in the managing director's office, still unsure how I was going to impart the bad news.

'How was the factory tour?', he opened.
'Very good', I replied.
'And how were my people?', he asked.
'Well, they are all very enthusiastic', I replied, 'but there is one problem. They don't think you have a strategy!'

> There was a silence. Then the MD got up and walked to the bookcase, took a thick binder and dropped it on the desk facing me. On the front was written 'Company Strategy'. So he had one.
>
> He slowly opened the file and on the front page were his name and his signature. He had written the documents some two months earlier. But above his name and his signature, were the names and signatures of all eight of his direct reports. They had all signed the documents in the last six weeks.

The story in the example above illustrates a number of points.

In most organisations the strategy is not understood or communicated. It is often written, consigned to a bookcase and brought out again the next year when it needs to be updated. In this case the managing director had gone further than this. He had written the strategy, but he had asked his direct reports to read and review it and then sign it. This they had duly done. But had they understood it? Had they agreed to it? Or had they simply done as they were asked? Certainly, from our conversation, it appeared that they had forgotten about the document.

So how can you overcome this? You can do two things. Firstly, you have to engage the senior team in the decision-making. Secondly, you have to translate the strategy into a set of performance measures.

Engaging the team is critically important and the process we have described throughout this book is directed to encouraging that engagement. People need to debate the strategy, what it is based on and what it means for the organisation. The debate is central to the strategy formulation process and helps understanding, creates clarity and fosters commitment. So the development of strategy should never be delegated to an isolated staff team, as all of the above are lost.

Translating the strategy into a set of performance measures is a very important process. Firstly, it clarifies what is to be achieved by when – something often omitted from the strategy document.

Secondly, it communicates what the strategy is to those who have not been directly involved in strategy formulation, when they see new measures created and reported. By creating a set of measures and displaying them around the company, you are saying these things are important, because you are measuring them. You are also saying activities that are not being measured are less important. Creating a set of performance measures closely aligned to the strategy is an effective way of communicating that strategy right across the organisation. In effect, it makes the strategy live, long after the strategy document has been put back on the shelf.

But there is also a 'health warning'. If your performance measures do not reflect your strategy, your people are most likely to follow the measures and not the strategy. Therefore you must ensure that the measures always reflect the strategy and that when you update the strategy, the measures are also updated to reflect the change in direction.

In effect, updating your measures is a very effective way of communicating a new strategic direction throughout the business.

What are the processes for keeping the scorecard up to date?

There are four key processes that will help you to keep the scorecard up to date (see Figure 7.1). These are:

1. **Reviewing targets**. These need to be reviewed on a regular basis and updated to reflect normal annual budget increases, improving performance, changing customer requirements, and the results from competitor analysis or external benchmarking.
2. **Developing the measures**. The measures drive behaviour so they need to be revised from time to time to overcome dysfunctional behaviour and to reflect new circumstances.

3. **Reviewing measures**. The success map and measures need to change when the strategy changes.
4. **Challenging the strategy**. The initial success map reflects the assumptions and beliefs of the people who created it. However, once the measures have been implemented and used, you should use them to challenge the success map.

We will describe these in turn and provide examples of these different processes in action.

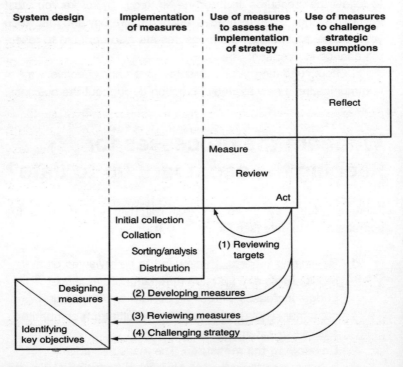

Figure 7.1: The process for keeping the Balanced Scorecard up to date

When do you update targets?

Accountants normally operate on an annual cycle, changing the budget at least once a year. This is minimum frequency for reviewing targets, as they should always be aligned to the budget. Targets need to be reviewed when an event triggers change, regardless of any other cycle.

Budgetary changes

Targets are updated annually during the normal budgeting process. It is usual for the sales income target for the next financial year to be reviewed. This will have to reflect inflation, increases and reductions in customer demand as well as the impact of competitor activity.

If you increase sales volumes, you will need to increase production output. This may require additional capacity or increased productivity. Ideally, the budgeting round cascades a series of changes through the organisation that reflect not only changes in the budget, but also in the non-financial performance measures. The annual budget cycle may be the trigger, but many organisations are moving to quarterly rolling budgets, requiring targets to be reviewed and updated much more frequently.

Performance improvement

Regularly attaining or surpassing a target suggests it needs to be reviewed and possibly revised. Here are two examples:

On-time delivery An instrument manufacturer regularly attained the 90% on-time target set for delivering orders to their customers on the day promised. As on-time delivery was highly valued by their customers, the target was increased to 95% for the following year.

The achievement of a target should automatically trigger a review of that target. However, it should not automatically trigger an increase in the target set. All improvements have an associated cost and you need to balance the cost against the business and customer benefits.

Pizza delivery A pizza company had a target of delivering all orders within 20 minutes of the order being taken. They reinforced the target by promising not to charge their customers if the delivery promise wasn't kept. Having reached an almost perfect on-time delivery performance within the 20 minutes, the company didn't reduce its target. 20 minutes was a reasonable time for the customer to wait and there was no overriding customer or business benefit from reducing the target. In fact the costs of providing the resources to deliver more quickly were simply prohibitive.

Customer needs

Customers will drive change in two situations. First, when an improved performance opens a new market opportunity for them and they require the better performance to exploit the situation. Secondly, when they respond positively to competitor improvements, you have to respond appropriately to keep their business.

External benchmark-driven changes

The sudden discovery that others' performance is better than yours will result in the review and possible change in targets.

> **Shock of benchmarking** Borealis (the Danish plastics company) used to set its cost targets based on the previous year's performance. An external benchmarking exercise revealed the company's performance wasn't quite as good as it expected. The targets then became set based on their performance against their key competitors'.

Strategy-driven changes

Creating and securing a strategic advantage is difficult. It can often be achieved only by delivering very high performance on a few specific performance measures. To do this, the change in target usually requires a significant change in the process for achieving that target.

> **Delivering strategic advantage** Milliken's industrial carpet business relied heavily on gaining specification through architectural practices. The vast majority of these were located in central London. As part of the strategy to increase specifications, Milliken wanted to improve their responsiveness to the architects. They had achieved a good response by using an overnight courier service but, ideally, architects wanted samples within a couple of hours of making a telephone call. They realised the overnight service didn't

provide a significantly better performance than their competitors'. Using motorbike couriers for key accounts was an option, but that would be expensive. The solution was to employ a van and driver. The van was stacked with all the samples and simply drove around central London all day responding to the latest requests. Architects were impressed that they could call in the morning and have their sample when they got back from lunch. This created a favourable impression, encouraged the architects always to request samples from Milliken, and resulted in increased specification of their products.

How do you update targets?

There are two factors that need to be considered in target setting. One is based on Motivation Theory (Theory M), the other is based on Process Theory (Theory P).

Theory M suggests that all targets should be 'high but attainable'. This is based on decades of motivation research showing that people respond best to targets, which they believe that the can reach, but stretch their performance almost to the limit. How you do this in practice is not so easy. You can involve people in setting the target and you can use your own judgement and experience. But be aware of the consequences especially if you attach some form of financial reward to the target.

Rewarding failure   A drug company had an exceptional portfolio of existing products that were market leaders. The company focused resources on promotion of new drugs coming to the market with one key manager handling the sales and marketing effort for existing drugs. When negotiating her targets for 2007, she claimed that with a small increase in budget, she could increase the sales volumes for the next year by some 50 per cent. Unfortunately, her boss accepted the target. We joined the conversation a year later, when she had achieved a 45 per cent improvement, but had missed her target and the accompanying bonus. The conversation about the 2008 target was stalled. She wanted a target of 5 per cent increase in sales, her boss was trying to push for 10 per cent. So often we see systems where the target-setting process results in people trying to minimise the target so they can achieve it, whilst their bosses are trying to extend the target. This situation results in information becoming so valuable that the two parties don't share it. Trust is undermined and business development can be badly affected. What would have been the situation if the drug company had recognised the exceptional performance from the previous year and acted accordingly?

Theory P comes from a completely different angle. This is based on the belief that performance improvement comes from changes in processes and not from getting people to work hard. This is based on the assumption that a process has a natural level of performance as made explicit through the process charts described in Chapter 6. Target setting should then be based on external comparison; either by comparing performance with competitors, or from quantifying the customers' requirements.

Improvements in performance come from improvements in processes. Unlike motivational based improvements, these are usually sustainable.

Planning improvement A planning department was struggling to achieve the government target for turning round plans in the prescribed number of days. An external review suggested an increase in the number of planning staff. The council involved was concerned about the additional cost this would bring, so commissioned a review of the process. By streamlining the process so a central team answered simple queries and planners were not interrupted by routine enquires, the performance improved and the target was met.

To summarise, staff need to be motivated so they strive to improve performance and targets can help in achieving this. But sustainable improvements in performance come ultimately from *what* we do. In planning improvement, you should also plan and deliver the changes to processes by which improved performance will be delivered.

Revising the measures

There is another conflict in performance measurement. On the one hand, you need stable measures to track longer-term trends and changes in performance over time. On the other hand, you need to change the scope and definitions as circumstances change.

Change is needed when the measure:

● is simply wrong or can now be improved in light of experience;
● is causing people to play games;
● needs to be broadened to extend its scope;
● needs to be adapted to changing circumstances.

Most measures will be found wanting when they are first installed. The baggage handlers' example in Chapter 4 is a classic example and eventually the airport developed a system for recording the time to the last bag. This reflected what the passengers wanted and overcame the 'gaming' of the measure being conducted by the ground crew.

You need to adapt your measures as your business develops. For example, you may start by measuring the on-time delivery of your core product range. Then you find that, over time, your core product is becoming a smaller part of the whole business. So you have to revise the performance measures and broaden the scope to include the emerging products. But you must not forget to do this, as the staff concerned will be content to leave the existing measure as it is.

Revising measures as needs change can best be explained by an example.

The suggestion scheme A Japanese car manufacturer wanted to increase the number of suggestions it received from its UK workforce, so it implemented a measure of the number of suggestions received. Over the next couple of months the number of suggestions rapidly increased, but there was now a bottleneck in the engineering department reviewing the suggestions. As a result, the key measure was revised to 'the number of suggestions reviewed'. Doing this moved the focus of the measurement away from the workforce making the suggestions to the efficiency of the review process. In a few weeks, this started to improve, but the company was now interested in the quality of the suggestions received. So the definition changed. The measure became the percentage of suggestions accepted. But having the suggestion accepted didn't mean it was implemented, so a further redefinition was required. The 'number of suggestions implemented' became the key measure. Finally, someone suggested that the real measure should be the benefit accrued to the company in terms of cost saving. As someone then asked, 'how did we get here?'

In the example above, the measures had to be changed as the requirement had changed. However, the company could not have started with the final measure because, if they had done this, they would never have created the behaviour that allowed them to reach their final goal.

The performance measure record sheet (described in Chapter 4) is a useful tool for revising the performance measures as it makes people work though the questions they need to ask to develop an appropriate measure at the outset.

Reviewing the measures

Maintaining the old scorecard is a recipe for ensuring any new strategy is never implemented. When your strategy changes, your measures need to be changed to reflect those changes. If this is not done, a misalignment will develop between the strategy and the scorecard. The success map should be revisited at least once a year.

Here is an example. If a company is moving from competing on cost to competing on responsiveness, the scorecard needs to change. This will mean dropping some existing measures and introducing new ones. At first glance this change looks to be simple, but there is usually a whole set of entrenched performance measures which will work against it. To be cost competitive in a manufacturing setting, machine utilisation is important and so is labour efficiency. Longer production runs, minimising the changeover costs and gaining all the benefits from stable production will achieve this. Responsiveness, on the other hand, requires excess capacity and under-utilised resources to provide the flexibility the customers now need. It requires smaller job lots and batch sizes.

Implementing a measure of responsiveness, such as 'reduction in average lead-time' at the top level, may well suggest you are implementing your strategy, but if you do not remove the supporting process measures such as 'labour utilisation' and 'machine efficiency', the behaviour in the production area will not change. The lower level measures must align with the new strategy. If they do not, the chain in the success map will be broken and the strategy will remain a pipe dream. As the strategy changes, you must change the measures right down the organisation, removing those measures that conflict with the new strategy.

Rebuilding the success map asking the 'what?' and 'how?' questions we saw in Chapter 3 will help you do this. You should also challenge this analysis by asking 'why?'. 'Why are you are doing something?' Does this link to what you are trying to achieve at the higher level?

Challenging strategy

When you build a success map you rely on the teams' understanding of the business and the collective experience and assumptions about how the business works. Sometimes these are correct, but often when assumptions are tested using the data collected for the performance measure you find something has been missed. That is an opportunity to learn.

The classic case is presented in *Harvard Business Review* and relates to Sears Roebuck and Company. In the mid-1990s, they looked at how their employee satisfaction had an impact on their customer satisfaction, and on how their customer satisfaction had an impact on their sales revenues and financial performance. But unlike many companies who made this link, they collected the data from around their stores right across the country and tested the hypothesis. This meant they could predict the impact of a five unit increase in employee satisfaction on customer impression and financial performance.

You could understand the link between employee and customer satisfaction in retailing, because many employees are in face-to-face contact with customers. But interestingly it holds in other businesses too. Clive Jeanes (formerly MD of Milliken in Europe) used to explain that, in his capital intensive business, there was about an 18-months delay between a fall in customer satisfaction and a downturn in financial performance. He also showed a relationship between employee satisfaction and customer satisfaction, although the relationship was weaker, there was a 12-month delay in this case.

Challenging strategy A chairman of a UK bank presented his results at one of the shareholders meetings. He finished the presentation by explaining how he believed that happy employees made happy customers, and how happy customers created better financial returns. He was rather surprised by the first question from one of the analysts who asked:

'Mr Chairman, where does your company sit in the *Sunday Times'* list of best employers?'

The Chairman didn't know about the Sunday Times list, so couldn't answer the question. The analyst was just doing his job – finding out how committed the company was to the strategy they espoused.

Marcus Buckingham and Curt Coffman at Gallup have shown a relationship between employee satisfaction and attributes of business performance across a wide range of businesses in the United Kingdom and United States, but we would argue that you should use your own data to test your own success map.

Late planes BA have measured customer satisfaction over a number of years, but they had not tested whether their customer satisfaction policy had a positive impact on performance. Dr Mohammad Al-Najjar and Prof. Andy Neely were given access to five years' worth of customer satisfaction data and used this to test statistically the customer satisfaction strategy.

Their data showed that indeed, financial performance was significantly and positively related to the customers' 'willingness to recommend BA to friends and colleagues'. They also found that 'willingness to recommend' was positively and significantly related to 'customer satisfaction'. So that part of the model worked.

So what was the driver of 'customer satisfaction'? From the data, 'cabin crew service' was the only significant factor. But what was influencing 'cabin crew service'? Here they found three factors. 'Satisfaction with check-in' and 'meal rating' were two obvious drivers of customer satisfaction. If the passengers were upset at check-in they would not be well disposed towards the airline. Similarly, the meal is the main point of interaction between the cabin crew and the passengers. But the third result was unexpected. 'Departure on time' was significantly but negatively correlated to 'customer satisfaction'.

That meant that every time a BA plane left late, cabin crew service was better, customer satisfaction increased, willingness to recommend rose and BA made more money!

Now that seems counterintuitive until you reflect on what happens when a plane is delayed. The delay is often not BA's fault. Catering, air traffic control, late arrival of the flight can all be causes not attributable by passengers to BA. Also, when the flight is delayed, the captain has the opportunity to communicate to the passengers and to keep them informed of the situation. The cabin crew also have an incentive to welcome you on board. Besides having more time, they want you to relax so that they can have a quiet flight. A little customer care whilst the departure is being delayed can go a long way later.

The answer was that service recovery compensates for most of the BA's departure delays. It revealed how important the cabin crew service was at that time and how it had an impact on customer satisfaction and then on financial results. The message for BA was not 'how do we get all our flights to leave late?' but 'how do we get our cabin crew service to be a little better when there is no delay?'

If you use your performance measurement data to test your success map we would be surprised if you didn't find an anomaly as in the BA case above. Nearly every company we know that has tested their success map has found something that, on first inspection, they did not understand. This is where you are challenging your assumptions. The outcome gives you a chance to spot something you did not know and to learn from it. Many companies have swallowed the 'happy employees make happy customers make happy shareholders' mantra, but testing this with your own data should prove very rewarding.

So we have described how you need to review the targets, the measures, the set of measures and the strategy itself. In the next section we will touch on some of the barriers to doing this.

What are the barriers to be overcome?

We have included here a checklist showing the types of barriers that need to be overcome.

1. **The reward system.** The problem with the reward system is that it can ossify the Balanced Scorecard. When you align the incentives and bonus payments to the Balanced Scorecard, it certainly makes people pay attention, but it can make the measures difficult to change. Increasing targets from one year to the next will meet with resistance as this means the target is harder to reach. Also, it may result in staff playing games with the target, just achieving the target so the bonus is paid, but not over-achieving in case the target is raised significantly the next year. When this happens right across the company, it will cause significant performance

issues. Also, changing the measures included in the bonus system will cause concern amongst staff. They become accustomed to the measures used in the bonus and will develop strategies for achieving them. Making a change will therefore be resisted.

2. **Functional comparisons**. Many larger companies are structured into business units. But they often have main board directors who have functional responsibilities for activities such as sales, marketing, operations, HR and finance. The problem is that these directors may use their own measures of success to compare the performance of different parts of the business. In operations, plant utilisation is regularly used as a measure, but if the local business unit is competing on flexibility, plant utilisation may well not be the most important measure to use. This conflict between head office and local priorities can result in measures not being changed, or worse, two conflicting sets of measures being used.

3. **Comfort zones**. Why change? People get comfortable with the measures they know and it takes time and effort to update them.

4. **IT systems**. Unfortunately, updating the measure may well require changes to the data capture or calculations. In one company we know, an on-time delivery measure was delayed for several months whilst the company waited for the next release of the software needed to calculate it.

5. **Management time**. There is always pressure on management time, and reviewing the measurement system can be overlooked and even forgotten. Those involved in updating the strategy may think their job is complete when that part is done. We have come across organisations that have then failed to communicate the new direction as they have not reviewed and rolled out the new measures.

Conclusion

In this chapter we have focused on how important it is to keep your Balanced Scorecard and your measures up to date. Most companies have a cycle of reviewing their performance, but you will need to introduce processes to ensure your targets, measure definitions, sets of measures and strategies are regularly reviewed. These should not all be done at the same time, but we would recommend that each of these processes should have been used at least once over the course of a year.

INSTANT TIP

Don't let the scorecard become out of date. It will either fall into disrepute or suffocate strategy implementation.

08

How can you apply the Balanced Scorecard in different settings?

Introduction

In this chapter we will describe how you can apply the Balanced Scorecard in different settings. We will start by tackling the issue of how to create a Balanced Scorecard that operates across the different levels of a business. We will then look at the issue of support functions (such as HR, finance, maintenance), where you are trying to align the activity of the function with the performance of the business. Finally, we will touch on the use of the Balanced Scorecard in the public and 'not-for-profit' sectors.

Cascading the Balanced Scorecard

The Balanced Scorecard originally had its origins in creating a performance measurement dashboard for a business unit. A business unit is a relatively homogeneous organisation that has customers and usually operates as a profit centre. Most small companies comprise a single business unit, but it is also possible to have a very large company operating as a single business unit. The approach to creating a scorecard that we described in Chapter 3 assumes this.

But what happens if you are not developing a scorecard for a business unit? What happens if the business units form part of a larger organisation with a divisional structure? What happens if you want to cascade the Balance Scorecard to the functional departments?

We will address these issues here.

Branch structures

You only have to walk down the high street of any large town to see the local branches of larger businesses. The high street banks and retail outlets are ubiquitous, as are the fast food outlets, coffee shops and estate agents. But go off the high street just a little way and you will run into branches of national builders' merchants, specialist car repairers, hotel chains and even serviced office suppliers. Many large organisations have branch networks, or operate a franchise service, which appears as though they have a branch network.

So how do you create a Balanced Scorecard for a branch network?

One way of doing this is by treating the branch as the business unit. By analysing the customers' requirements and merging these with the requirements of the owners and other important stakeholders, you can create a success map that applies to any of the branches in your network. Assuming that all the branches are very similar, you can deploy the same set of measures to all the branches. You can compare the performance of the different branches by their scorecards, and even create league tables of how well different branches are doing on different measures. You can then add up the performances of all the branches in a region, to create a regional scorecard, and you can add these regions up to create a business scorecard.

Creating a scorecard for a branch network can have many advantages:

1. Because all the branches are very similar, you can create a single scorecard that applies across all the branches. This means management time invested in creating that scorecard is well spent as it can be applied in multiple situations.
2. Most organisations want their customers to receive the same level of service at all their branches. The scorecard can reinforce this by measuring the key attributes of customer service against centrally set target levels.
3. Branches can be compared in league tables. This can create friendly rivalry, although it has to be managed carefully. The scorecard can also be used to identify best practice and motivate branch managers to improve the running of their part of the business.

However, there are a couple of issues to watch:

1. Be careful, as it is not possible to set the same targets for all branches. Your customer service targets may all be the same, but targets for turnover, profitability and return on investment will have to be set to reflect the local circumstances. If they do not, branch managers may not react positively to the scorecard.
2. You may have great efficiencies from creating a single scorecard that applies to all your branches, but do not forget that local buy in will be required if the scorecard is

going to be successful. You will need to invest time and effort to do this.

Getting the buy in   The division of a builders' merchant set out to create a Balanced Scorecard. This started with an introduction to performance measurement for the directors and senior managers at which the Balanced Scorecard was discussed, together with the approach that would be used to create and deploy a scorecard in their business. Following this initial launch, a smaller group comprising the directors and divisional managers worked together through a series of workshops, creating and refining their success map. Once this was agreed in outline, the results were presented back to the regional managers who were encouraged to review and critique what had been developed. This cemented the support for the scorecard at the senior level, but the approach still had to be rolled out to the branches. A conference was arranged with all branch managers and the new measurement system was presented. But this was only the start of the process: to ensure that all the branch managers in the business understood the scorecard, a 'train the trainer' programme was developed. Senior managers were trained to train the branch managers, and the branch managers were trained to train their own staff. In this way the scorecard was rolled out across an organisation with over several hundred branches.

Dumping the scorecard on others   I worked for an international airline catering company with kitchens at Heathrow and Gatwick airports. One day we received a set of new performance measures from head office and were asked to report regularly on them.

In one kitchen, the measures were simply passed to the relevant managers, the data collected and reported back. In fact, very little changed.

In the other kitchen, the management team was annoyed with the imposition of the measures. We had a meeting and decided we could do better ourselves. So we set up a couple of half-day workshops where we looked at our business, how it was structured and what we should measure and report. At the end of the second workshop we compared what we had developed with what had been sent from head office. There were differences, but we soon realised that the differences were really very minor and we finally adopted the head office set of measures for running the business. We then deployed these measures to the various departments and reviewed our results in the management meetings on a weekly basis. Performance started to improve, and we published the results around the business. Interestingly, in this kitchen, the initial annoyance with the imposition of the measures from head office had created a process that allowed us to question and then understand why the new measures were appropriate. This process created the buy in that led to the performance measures being used to run the business very effectively.

If you create branch scorecards that roll up to form regional scorecards and eventually to a business wide scorecard, you must always consider whether other factors need to be included at the corporate business level. Branch scorecards will reflect how the business operates, but there are usually other issues that need to be added at the corporate level.

Firstly, the business will have central support functions. These may include a central buying function, an HR department and an accounting and finance function. You will have to decide if you want to create scorecards for these departments, or risk people seeing them as being 'too lofty to be measured'. We describe how to create support function scorecards later in this chapter.

Secondly, there may be activities that are conducted at the business level but not in the branches. The management of key accounts may fall into this category, as will the management of key suppliers. In this situation, the branch scorecard may provide a useful point to start the process, but you will have to review the activities of the business in its wider setting before settling on a business level scorecard.

Cascading the scorecard down the organisation

Many organisations do not have a branch structure. In this case, the business unit itself is often structured functionally into sales and marketing, operations, product development, finance and HR. This necessitates the development of different scorecards for the different functions.

In our experience, the most effective way of doing this is to create success maps for each of the functions.

EDF Energy   EDF Energy, who operate in the South and East of England, distribute electricity to over a quarter of the UK population. Each year EDF Energy's networks branch creates a success map and a scorecard based on the company's ambitions. Once this is created, it is cascaded to the next level. Each of the business units then takes the branch strategy map and uses it as the starting point for developing their own strategy map and scorecard. Using a similar process, they develop their objectives and measures so that they align with and support the branch goals. This process is then repeated with the functions and teams (see Figure 8.1).

NHBC NHBC (the National House-Building Council) provides warranties on new homes in the UK. As part of its activities, it also inspects the building of new homes and provides building control services. Creating a scorecard for NHBC has involved engaging each of the main service functions in developing their own success map. The claims team has created a success map that explicitly explained and measured how they contributed to NHBC's success through the efficient and effective handling of customers and builders as well as the insurance claims. Similarly, success maps have been created for the inspection teams, building control teams and customer service teams.

Cascading the scorecard down the organisation by creating sets of success maps at different levels is a time-consuming process. However, the approach has all the benefits of engaging with those managing the business. It creates an understanding of their objectives and how they fit into the objectives of the business. If you adopt this approach you will foster ownership of the success maps and the performance measures.

To quote Mark Bromley, Head of Business Performance of EDF Energy: 'By taking a facilitated approach, I get 80% of the measures I want and 100% of the buy in. If I simply told them what to measure, I might get all the measures I want, but only 10% of the commitment to use them.'

Divisions and subsidiary companies

In a branch network it is usually the case that all the branches are doing similar activities, serving similar customers and following a single strategy. However, in many organisations, the corporate

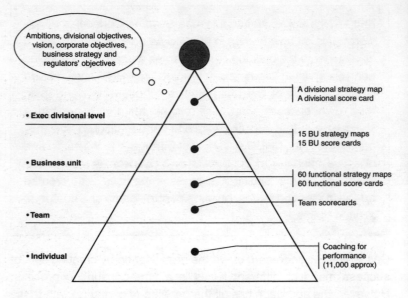

Figure 8.1: How EDF Energy cascade their scorecard (Adapted from Martinez et al, 2006)

structure is very different. At the extreme, all the subsidiary companies have their own customers and strategies, and the principal role of head office is to provide finance and management control.

Obviously if all the companies are in the situation of managing their own destiny with little or no direction from the centre, then there is no need to have a Balanced Scorecard that is cascaded from one level in the organisation to the next. Most conglomerates in this situation simply ask for financial information to be provided on a regular basis, and occasionally key indicators of risk and compliance, such as health and safety figures or brand loyalty.

The norm, however, is where there is some alignment or co-ordination between the subsidiaries, and this is where the scorecard can help develop an understanding of exactly what is required, and how much freedom of action subsidiary companies have.

Allowing for difference An electronics company supplied Europe. The head office was in the UK, but there were four regions and subsidiary companies operating in each of the main countries. In creating a scorecard, we built a success map that described in principle what the organisation had to do to be successful. However, there were key differences in how this would be implemented in the different countries. At the time, in the UK, the internet was becoming an extremely important route to market. In other countries, developing the dealer network was much more important.

The solution was to create a scorecard that had common objectives and some common measures. For example, all the financial objectives and measures were common between the head office, region and country, as were the HR and people development measures and measures of customer satisfaction. There were then common objectives around developing channels to market, but the measures used for each country were developed specifically to align with the local strategy. In this way, we differentiated between those objectives that everyone in the group were charged with fulfilling and those over which local management had discretion.

As the group managing director put it: 'I now have a framework that allows me to have a structured conversation about performance with any of my regional directors or any of my country managers.'

So, in developing a scorecard across divisions and subsidiary companies, it is important to define the role of the centre and of the subsidiary. Making all subsidiaries use the same set of measures can be counter-productive because the measures should reflect the strategic imperatives at the level of the organisation to which they are applied. The trick here is to balance the parent organisation's need for homogeneity across its business with the level of local discretion you are going to allow in order to compete with local competition.

Support functions

The first question that is often asked is 'should we measure our support functions' performance?' Every organisation we have dealt with has come to the conclusion that support functions should be treated in the same way as the rest of the business.

Aligning support functions with the rest of the business can be a challenge. Firstly, they do not always see how they fit in. Secondly, they often see their world in terms of their own functional specialism. Thirdly, there can be a real tension between how much the support function wants to spend and how much the functions being supported want to pay. Most support functions want to give a 'Rolls Royce' service, but this comes at a cost that other parts of the organisation do not want to bear.

We will describe two approaches here. The first approach is to create a simple scorecard by working with support function managers and considering the following questions:

1. What does the internal customer require from you and how will they measure your performance?
2. How will you know whether you are going to deliver what the internal customer requires and how will you measure this?
3. What services are you reliant on from other departments (including the internal customer) to deliver your service and how will you measure this?
4. What are the financial constraints and how will you measure these?
5. What skills and resources will you require to deliver the service and how will you measure this?

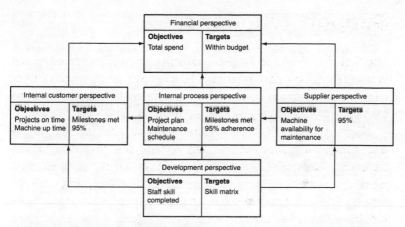

Figure 8.2: A maintenance scorecard

Figure 8.2 provides an example of a scorecard developed from taking this approach, but if you can only involve the service function managers without their internal customers you may still encounter the three challenges we outlined above.

The second approach is to create a success map. This overcomes most of the issues raised above by involving the support function managers and their internal customers. Figure 8.3 shows an example created for a maintenance function, which supported three operating units. In this case, the operating units were unhappy with the support they were receiving and the maintenance function felt unable to maintain the equipment properly.

The maintenance success map We started the process by asking the internal customer – in this case the production department – to identify their key objectives. These were output, quality and on-time delivery. We then asked them to highlight the key contribution the maintenance function made to achieving these goals. Maximising plant availability was identified as being the key contribution. Having established a dialogue between the two groups, we asked the maintenance team to create a success map to describe how this would be achieved. By engaging both the customer and the supplier in these debates, both gained an understanding of the other's point of view Issues were raised, including maintenance's concern that they were not always given access to the plant to do their work at the times planned, and the reliance on other departments for information, the sales forecast being the most important in this case.

Finally, we ran into the issue of the cost of maintenance. We resolved this by creating two factors that had to be balanced, the cost of lost production and the maintenance cost per tonne produced. Production had always complained about the cost of maintenance but had never considered the costs the organisation was incurring when the equipment was down. Maintenance had always provided a service, but had never had a guide as to how cost effective they were. Using the two cost indicators and keeping the 'maximising plant availability' objective in mind, we created a means of measuring the interface between the production operation and its support maintenance service. The success map we produced enabled both parties to understand how each had an impact on the other.

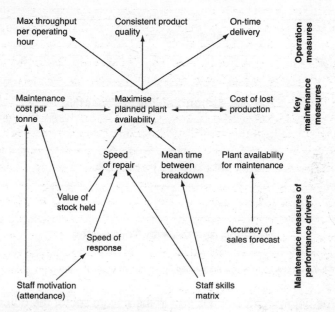

Figure 8.3: Maintenance department success map.

Balanced Scorecard in the public and 'not-for-profit' sectors

Performance Measures in the public sector are very much in the public eye. School league tables, survival rates for surgery and detection rates for crime are frequently reported and commented upon. Measures are used for a variety of purposes – many of which are akin to those in the commercial sector – but some of which may be more connected with public relations. There are certainly sensitivities in the public sector to which most private sector organisations are not normally subjected.

Balanced Scorecards are used in the public sector. The way they are developed is by amending the presentation of the perspectives so the customer perspective appears at the top (see Figure 8.4)

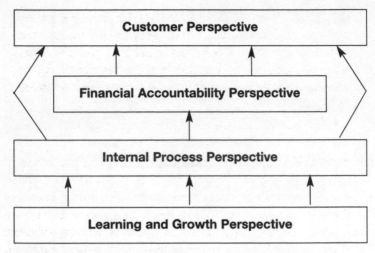

Figure 8.4: The basic format of the Balanced Scorecard for public services

The biggest difference is that in the private sector the outcome of all the Balanced Scorecard activity is profits and returns for the owners or shareholders, whilst in the public sector, the emphasis is on getting the best outcomes for the customers (dare we say stakeholders) whilst operating within a limited financial budget.

The real difficulty with the Balanced Scorecard is that it is not a multiple stakeholder framework and so doesn't lend itself easily to many public sector situations. The Performance Prism (which we will describe in Chapter 9) explicitly deals with multiple stakeholders and therefore adapts to use in the public sector more easily.

Who is the customer?   Take a simple example of the prison service. Who is the customer? Is it the prisoners themselves who have committed the crimes? Is it the judiciary who have sent the individuals to gaol? Is it the government who have a policy of reducing crime? Or is it the general public who want to feel safer at home?

In fact all of these groups have a stake in the prison service and you could look at their requirements through the Balanced Scorecard framework above. But it is clear that wants and needs are very different and often conflicting so you need a process of creating a scorecard that resolves these issues.

One of the key difficulties faced by managers in the public sector is that they have targets imposed on them by government. These are national targets and may or may not be appropriate at a local level. This is compounded in the local government setting by various government departments and agencies wanting different information from different departments within the local authority. Creating a top-level scorecard for a local authority then becomes extremely difficult, as there are so many competing demands.

In the 'not-for-profit' sector, most organisations will find that their scorecard will follow the example shown in Figure 8.4. But there are two important points to note.

1. When you undertake a review of customers' requirements, you must remember that your organisation is not there to deliver all the customers' needs. Therefore you should identify precisely which of the requirements you will endeavour to provide for and those you will not. You should make this very explicit to everyone involved so that the focus is clear. It will also remove hours of wasted argument.

2. A recent piece of research has shown that donors are increasingly asking for their own measures of performance as a prerequisite for the donation. Be very careful in this situation, as it will create a plethora of measures that confuse staff and undermine the performance of the organisation.

The tools and approaches we describe in this book are useful in the public and 'not-for-profit' sectors. Many of the issues are the same and the rigour of working through the processes with some commonsense adaptations is worthwhile. However, if your organisation is operating within these two sectors you should strongly consider the Performance Prism approach described in Chapter 9.

Conclusion

In this chapter we have described how the Balanced Scorecard can be used in a variety of organisational settings including single business units and groups of companies. We have also described how it should be cascaded down the organisation and applied to support service functions. Finally, we touched on the issues raised by the public and 'not for profit' sectors.

In the next chapter we will look at two other frameworks – the Performance Prism (which is particularly useful as an alternative to the Balanced Scorecard in a complex multi-stakeholder environment) and the process framework (which integrates the scorecard with your business processes).

INSTANT TIP

Adapt the scorecard to your situation and cascade it down the organisation.

09

What are the alternatives?

Introduction

The Balanced Scorecard is certainly very popular, but it does have its shortcomings. In this chapter we will start by taking a critical look at the Balanced Scorecard before presenting two additional frameworks that are more useful in specific situations.

The first of these frameworks is the Performance Prism, which takes a multi-stakeholder approach to performance measurement and management. The second is the Process Framework, which is important for use in the operations of your organisation. We will also show you how this framework can be integrated with the Balanced Scorecard.

What is wrong with the Balanced Scorecard?

In the late 1980s when the first scorecard was created, there was a widespread fixation in business with measuring and managing financial performance. Companies were inward looking, often ignoring what was happening in the market place or not noticing the actions of their competitors. Most reporting systems were focused on the past – what happened last month, last quarter or last year – rather than looking forward to the future. In this situation, the promotion of the Balanced Scorecard was a breath of fresh air. It suggested that companies should look externally at how their shareholders and customers viewed the business, focus internally on excelling in key processes and develop approaches to innovate and learn. The framework was simple, having only four perspectives, and very seductively presented in a series of *Harvard Business Review* articles.

Today, arguments in favour of constructing non-financial measures are widely accepted. Participants attending workshops at Cranfield University invariably understand the potential pitfalls of managing through financial measures alone. They are more interested in how they can make the scorecard work in their own organisation and how they should build success maps that link the perspectives together and assist in translating strategy into action. However, in doing this few of us rarely stop to criticise the Balanced Scorecard itself and to ask if it is still valid ten years after its inception.

So what criticisms can be made of the Balanced Scorecard?

1. **People are excluded.** Although many companies implementing the Balanced Scorecard translate the Innovation and Learning Perspective into a people perspective, the people perspective was not included in the 1992 *Harvard Business Review* version of the scorecard. We would highly recommend adopting a people perspective for two reasons. Firstly, people make the major contribution to improved performance as shown by the experience of companies such as Sears Roebuck and Milliken Europe as well in Lingle and Schiemann's study of the link between measurement and performance. Secondly, not measuring people gives the impression that they do not matter to the business, not something to promote when implementing a new way of working.

2. **Suppliers are excluded.** Many companies are dependent on their suppliers. Take financial services as an example. IT provision, application development and communication networks are being increasingly outsourced, but they are still critical to business success. In manufacturing companies, the biggest spend is often with external suppliers of materials, parts and components. Scorecard proponents argue that suppliers should be considered within the process perspective, but in most organisations this approach does not give suppliers the visibility they now deserve.

3. **Regulators are ignored.** Companies are being subjected to regulation. The FDA has an immense impact on the fortunes of drug companies, the FAA on aviation, the FSA on financial services and the Health and Safety Executive on nearly every business. But besides these very obvious regulators there are both statutory and self-regulatory rules, which must be complied with on everything from capital sufficiency to money laundering. These are non-negotiable standards which have to be met, but do not fit easily into the Balanced Scorecard framework.

4. **Community and environmental issues are missing.** Many companies may believe these are not important to them, but several high-profile cases should make them at least consider this perspective. Most of us cannot forget Union Carbide's disaster in Bhopal, when many people were killed. BP more recently has had safety problems in the United States, so obvious environmental and safety issues come to mind. But there are other issues arising from 'people pressure'. Shell, despite their scientific risk assessment, ran into serious problems in disposing of their platform 'The Brent Spar' in the North Sea. Similarly, many UK retail banks have come under intense pressure in recent years as a direct result of their programmes to rationalise their branch networks. Environmental issues

and local communities are closely linked and companies need to measure and monitor the impact they are having. If they do not, they may find themselves subject to attack by pressure groups that can damage their reputation, interrupt trading and ultimately destroy their business.

5. **Competitors are ignored.** The Balanced Scorecard gives a perspective on the external environment through the eyes of shareholders and customers. Besides the stakeholders identified above, companies need to monitor the environment to track competitor activity and developments in technology. In this respect, it can be argued that the scorecard is not a truly strategic measurement framework because it only focuses on 'translating the strategy into action' – the implementation of the strategy. The scorecard is designed to answer the question 'is the chosen strategy being implemented?' It doesn't highlight or track threats from non-traditional competitors.

These criticisms mainly stem from the fact that the Balanced Scorecard is not a multiple stakeholder framework. There is an argument in academia over whether companies should be maximising profit or taking a more inclusive approach. This debate has spilled over into practice with companies such as Stern Stewart & Co promoting EVA™ (Economic Value Added) as the measure most closely related to shareholders' needs, whilst other organisations, such as Tomorrow's Company, are arguing for a much more inclusive approach. Whatever the merits of these arguments, in most western societies, other stakeholders cannot be ignored because, inevitably, their action will impact on financial performance and shareholder value. Therefore any performance measurement framework needs to reflect stakeholders' needs, even if this is in addition to the core success map.

Will the scorecard survive? Yes, we believe so because there are too many advantages to having a multi-dimensional framework for measuring performance. Financial results can be related to actions taken inside the business and so help us manage the business better in the future. Looking externally as well as internally means we are less likely to be surprised by changes in customer requirements or the emergence of a new competitor. This is something traditional budgeting and accounting never gave us.

Will the scorecard look the same in ten years time? Probably not; it already has changed significantly with the introduction of success maps and it will change again. The stakeholder movement is too strong to be ignored with huge power being transferred to people with the growth of the internet, the influence of the media and regulation. There is already an alternative stakeholder approach available in the form of the Performance Prism, which is gaining popularity, and we think it is inevitable the scorecard will adapt too.

The Performance Prism

The Performance Prism (Neely et al., 2002) is a framework developed jointly between Accenture, the international consulting firm, and the Centre for Business Performance at Cranfield School of Management. The Performance Prism is explicitly a multi-stakeholder framework, and so has uses both in the public and the private sector.

There are five facets to the Performance Prism:

- Stakeholder requirements
- Strategy
- Process
- Capability and resources
- Our requirements from the stakeholders.

Figure 9.1 outlines the framework in more detail.

The starting point for the Performance Prism is the stakeholder, not the strategy. So, through asking a series of questions, you can translate the stakeholders' requirements into strategy and then align the processes and resources. The final question to ask is 'what do we require back from our stakeholders?' Table 9.1 contains nine questions.

Stakeholders	Who are our stakeholders? What do our stakeholders require?
Strategy	Which of these wants and needs are we going to satisfy? What strategies are we going to pursue to satisfy these requirements?
Processes	What processes do we need to deliver these strategies? Are these processes capable of delivering the strategy?
Capabilities nd Resources	What capabilities and resources are required to make these processes perform effectively? Are we protecting, sustaining or developing these capabilities and resources appropriately?
Stakeholders	What do we require from our stakeholders?

Table 9.1: The questions to ask when developing a Performance Prism

As with the Balanced Scorecard, you should use the questions to create a success map that links together the assumptions and objectives. In that way you will develop a tool that is extremely powerful to communicate both within the executive and across the organisation.

The real strengths of the Performance Prism are as follows:

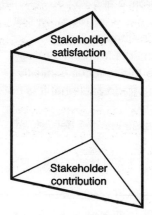

Stakeholders include

Investors

Customers and intermediaries

Employees

Regulators and communities

Suppliers

Three internal facets of the performance prism

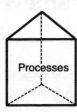

- Corporate
- Business unit
- Brands/products/
  services
- Operating

- Develop products
  and services
- Generate demand
- Fulfil demand
- Plan and manage
  enterprise

- People
- Practices
- Technology
- Infrastructure

Figure 9.1: The five facets of the Performance Prism (adapted from Neely et al, 2002)

1. It takes a multi-stakeholder approach and so you can use this approach to create success maps for the individual stakeholders (as we suggested in Chapter 3).
2. It separates stakeholder requirements from the strategy of the organisation. You can use this to focus explicitly on what the organisation is going to do and what it is not going to do.
3. It integrates the business processes into the delivery of performance.
4. It will help you align the capabilities and resources with the organisation's strategy.
5. It differentiates between what you want from your stakeholders and what they want from you.

The process framework

There is a wonderful quotation:

'You don't speed up your car by breaking the glass on the speedometer and pushing the indicator.'

A performance measure is exactly like the speedometer and, to continue the analogy, the scorecard is like the dashboard. Measurement enables reporting on performance improvement, it doesn't create it.

Performance improvement is only achieved by people in your organisation changing the way things are done. The scorecard tells them what is important and the targets also tell them what is to be achieved. So, for a time, simply measuring an aspect of performance may result in improvement because individuals give it more focus. However, if the performance improvement is to be sustained, then you will need to change the way the organisation works. This requires a change to your processes.

A good way of managing your organisation is to focus on your key processes. Typically, the key operating processes in a business unit are:

1. Win order (this will include everything from promoting your business, attracting customers and translating this activity into an order or a sale).
2. Fulfil order (this will include all the aspects of delivering the products or services customers have bought).
3. Develop product/service (this will include all the aspects of new product development and service redesign).
4. Support customer (this will include all aspects of the after sales service).

But each of these processes can be broken down into smaller processes. For example, you could subdivide the 'win order process' into:

(a) Attract customer interest (marketing).
(b) Convert interested customer enquiries into firm orders.

Similarly, you could subdivide the 'convert customer enquiry' process into:

(i) Understand customer requirements.
(ii) Produce quotation.
(iii) Close sale.

Processes are the building blocks that describe how your business works and you can map them from beginning to end. How far you need to break processes down will depend on their complexity and how you want to manage them. For process redesign, you may have to go beyond the third level, but for performance measurement processes, the second level is usually appropriate.

Performance is only improved by changing the processes, either directly or indirectly. Directly, means that you reconfigure the way things are done. Indirectly, means you may change the people, their skills, abilities or motivation. But to understand the performance of these processes and to gauge whether or not the changes you have made actually improve performance, you need to implement a measurement system.

Process measures can be separated into (see Figure 9.2):

- input measures
- process measures
- output measures
- outcome measures.

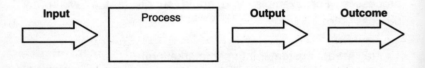

Figure 9.2: The basic process measurement framework

Let us take a sales process as an example – 'convert interested customer enquiries into firm orders'. The inputs are clearly the number of enquiries received and the outputs the number of firm orders placed. The outcomes refer to indirect consequences of this process. So one outcome will be sales turnover. But you may want to introduce other outcomes, such as satisfied customers, because these can be directly affected by the process. By selecting the outcomes, you are also signalling what is important to the company so you should choose these carefully.

You can choose the process measures to monitor the stages within the process, the quality of the process or the key resources that are available. For the process in our example you may consider the number of quotations produced to be important, the time from enquiry to quotation, the number of re-quotations (a possible source of waste or inefficiency), the number of sales staff available (see Figure 9.3).

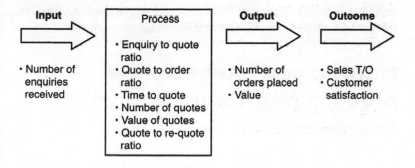

Figure 9.3: An example of measures for an order conversion process

By measuring the process in this way you can represent exactly what is happening. You might also use the SPC charts (described in Chapter 6) to represent the key measures.

The process framework then enables you to monitor the performance of the process as a whole and answer the following questions:

1. Is our enquiry rate increasing or falling?
2. Is the number/value of orders received increasing or falling?
3. Is our order conversion ratio, improving, staying constant or declining?
4. When enquiries increase, do we respond quickly enough?
5. Does our time to quote affect our rate of enquiry conversion?
6. How does the number of sales visits have an impact on our order conversion rate?
7. Is there a trend in the type of orders we are winning?
8. Have we provided the correct level of staff resource?

Many companies monitor their sales pipeline to judge the conversion rates at each stage of the sales process. By putting the measures into a framework and then displaying them in the format of Figure 9.3 above, you will be able to create a discussion with all levels of your sales team. These discussions invariably create new insights into the process and what is happening in the marketplace, allowing you to react and adapt to circumstance more quickly.

How do you integrate the process framework into your scorecard?

Given that processes are the building blocks of performance, it is important that you integrate them into the scorecard. You can achieve this by using the output and outcome measures from the process and plugging them directly into your scorecard. Figure 9.4 gives an example of how this may look in practice.

Conclusion

In this chapter we have been critical of the Balanced Scorecard. Our criticism is that it is not a multi-stakeholder framework. This makes it more inward looking and more focused on strategy implementation than other frameworks such as the Performance Prism. However, given the problem for most organisations is strategy implementation, and not strategy formulation, it is not surprising that the Balanced Scorecard is so widely used.

Improved performance doesn't come from measuring performance. Improved performance only comes from changing how you do things in your organisation. This is why it is important to link your process measures into the way you manage your business. So whichever approach you take, you should ensure that your business process measures align and feed into your scorecard.

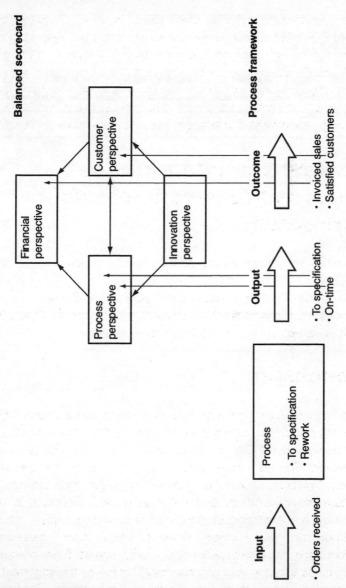

Figure 9.4: An illustration of the integration of the Balanced Scorecard with the process framework

INSTANT TIP

Don't forget the other stakeholders, such as the regulator and the community in which you operate – they can close your business.

10

How does a successful organisation change strategy into action?

Introduction

In this final chapter we will give a summary of the book with some practical hints from the perspective of those considering whether they should embark on a Balanced Scorecard project, those who are implementing their scorecard and those who are within an organisation where a scorecard is being implemented. We will draw these together with a case study from Tesco which has been using, very successfully, a version of the scorecard for the last ten years.

Should you use the Balanced Scorecard in your organisation?

If you want to:

- turn your strategy into action;
- ensure those actions happen;
- test whether your activities are achieving your organisation's objectives.

Then you should consider using the Balanced Scorecard. The process you undertake to construct your scorecard will involve an amount of rigour in testing existing assumptions about 'how things work' and will cause your management team and employees directly involved with particular activities (and therefore knowledge about them) to talk to each other. The debate, which may seem heated at times, should create new insights into the dynamics of your business.

The Balanced Scorecard works in most types of organisations – small or large – and for any sector. In the public and 'not-for-profit' sectors, the Performance Prism, described in Chapter 9, is a useful alternative because it is a multi stakeholder approach.

Above all, the Balanced Scorecard provides a framework for considering what the key objectives are for your organisation, what you need to do in order to achieve them (through the success mapping process) and how well you are progressing (through the reviews of your measures). You can adapt your scorecard to fit a whole business unit or a particular function or aspect of your business.

There are some questions you should ask before embarking on a Balanced Scorecard project:

- What is your overriding purpose for wanting to do it?
- Is the senior management team committed? If not, the project is unlikely to be as successful as it might be. You could waste a great deal of time.

- To what, exactly, will you apply your scorecard? Is it for a business unit, or the company as a whole? If you are considering a scorecard for more than one part of the business or organisation, how will these fit together, if at all?

The only cases in which we would strongly recommend you do not implement a Balanced Scorecard are when your organisation is in crisis or when you are operating in a very turbulent environment. Part of the beauty of the Balanced Scorecard is that it allows time for discussion and reflection. The measures themselves usually have a lead time and you will need time to establish some trends before taking action. At times of crisis, action is usually of the essence. Waiting and reflecting is not always appropriate.

Tips for creating a successful scorecard

We have described in this book a few key processes you might choose to follow in creating your scorecard. Although there are choices, there are some important factors for success:

- Consider in advance which process you will use for creating your scorecard.
- Communicate what the process is and involve people to get their buy-in; try to elicit what the benefits are for them.
- Assign a project co-ordinator to manage the creation and oversee the implementation.
- Maintain rigour in your process – although it is good to be flexible, if you keep changing the way things are done you will lose credibility.
- Keep your objectives firmly in mind.
- Be careful what you measure. 'What gets measured, gets done.' If you measure the wrong activities, you will cause

the wrong activities to happen.
- Make sure the measures you devise are really measuring what you want.
- Make sure your systems allow you to measure what you want.
- Keep your final scorecard as simple as possible.

Tips for using the scorecard effectively

There are many organisations with excellent looking scorecards but are they useful or have they become just another routine report to be done without any thought? The mechanisms for avoiding this are:

- Create at the outset a process and routine for reviewing the results from your scorecard and stick to it.
- Ask questions; make the scorecard a central topic of conversation.
- Make sure results are posted in a prominent position in a form people will understand.
- Be careful about causing rivalry between various parts of the organisation – you will encourage people to play games to avoid reporting accurately.
- Put individuals' names on your performance measure record sheet to make responsibility for action clear.
- Ensure actions are taken based on your reviews.
- Ensure your scorecard is adapted as circumstances change: if you do not do this you may find your strategy is pointing in one direction but all the activities in the other.

Tips for those being measured

The book has been written from the perspective of someone who is implementing or thinking about implementing the scorecard in his or her organisation. However, for each person implementing a scorecard there will be many more who are on the receiving end – those whose work is being measured. If you are in that position the key points to note are:

- Engage in the process. If your company is looking for volunteers, you should consider volunteering. You will then be on the inside and have a better chance to influence the process.
- Make your contributions from your own experience and knowledge, then you are more likely to be heard.
- Try to take an organisation-wide perspective; you cannot always look at the organisation from the perspective of your current job. Most of the benefits and improvements in performance come from helping departments work together; taking a wider perspective will improve these interfaces.
- If you become involved in an argument obtain the facts and figures to back up your position. Facts and figures are much more difficult to ignore than opinion.
- Ask questions when you do not understand. If you do not understand, it is probable that the rest of the organisation will have the same problem.
- Be prepared to argue over the setting of targets. Unfortunately too many organisations set targets by guesswork or by adding an arbitrary 10 per cent to last year's performance. You will have a problem if a bad target is set, but this will give the organisation a problem too.
- If a target looks too high, then ask how it is going to be achieved. If nothing is being changed, then you should

expect the existing trend to continue. If a target is out of line with this trend, it won't be reached unless a significant change is made.

- If meeting a target is dependent upon someone else delivering an activity, ensure that this is recorded. You might even consider introducing a measure that tracks the progress of your dependency so that it is visible for all to see.
- There will be things that are under your control, things you can influence and things that you can neither influence nor control. Focus your effort on the first two, as there are some things in life that you cannot change.
- Make sure you understand the process so you know when your issues or concerns should be raised. If you are not sure, then ask the facilitator and they should be able to help you. A good facilitator will want your points to be aired, so should help you to do just that.

Good advice We were once given some very good advice from the managing director of a company we were working with.

'If you don't like what is happening in your company, try and get involved in the change process. You will have a much better chance of influencing it from the inside. But once a decision has been made you have two stark choices. Either you commit to the change or you quickly find a new job. If you try and block a decision once it has been made then you should expect the company to get rid of you.'

Bringing it all together

The following is a case study from a very well known company, Tesco, which demonstrates very clearly how a seemingly complex business has adapted the Balanced Scorecard for its own use. As you will see from the description below, the scorecard plays a central role in the management and success of the business.

Tesco

The background

Tesco, one of the world's leading retailers. With a turnover of circa £42 billion worldwide, they are growing rapidly, expecting to create 25,000 new jobs in 2007. Their ethos is to keep things simple and this is reflected in their core purpose. Where many large companies will have a mission statement a paragraph long, followed by a page of values that no one can remember, Tesco states that its purpose is 'to create value for customers to earn their lifetime loyalty'. Tesco has just two key values, 'no-one tries harder for customers' and 'treat people as we like to be treated'. To some, the business may seem highly complex – 450,000 employees worldwide, a network of stores selling everything from groceries to jewellery and washing machines, not to mention a host of other services such as insurance and telecoms. But, somehow, Tesco seems to hold on to the idea that simplicity is best. This is reflected in the way they use a version of the Balanced Scorecard, which they call the steering wheel, to manage the business.

The steering wheel was introduced in the late 1990s with four perspectives – customer, financial, operations and people. However, in 2006 it was amended to add a fifth perspective, community, reflecting the changing environment in which the company was operating. Aware of pressure from customers, media and government, the company introduced an array of actions and measures such as reducing use of plastic bags and packaging, reduction of carbon emissions through use of bio fuels and trucks carrying double loads. There is also a 'good neighbour scheme' aimed particularly at the convenience stores, where noise pollution is being reduced through initiatives such as using cages with plastic bases and shelves which are significantly quieter than our old all-metal cages.

Communication

The company structure comprises a simple chain of command, with clear roles and people who know what is required of them. The steering wheel plays an important part in communicating direction throughout the organisation. The business plan is rolled out using the steering wheel and up to 50 per cent of the executive bonus is dependent on its results, so there is no doubt in employees' minds about its value. If a measure is set for reduction in queuing time then that is what will happen. The language used is simple and direct. They try to avoid acronyms and abbreviations to clarify communication. Given the connection between bonuses and results from the steering wheel, the measures agreed have to be fair, unambiguous and measurable. On this latter point, the target of having only one person in front in the checkout queue is measured by infra-red sensor.

Use of the steering wheel

There is a 'cascade' of the steering wheel, with a global, UK, store group and an individual wheel for each store. The measures and targets are tailored to the context in which it is being used – clearly Tesco Extra is not the same as an express store. There are no 'league tables' and the numbers are not intended to 'add up' but they do align. The measures and targets are set out in colourful documents that can be easily understood.

For such a large business, there are relatively few key measures, with the number going up from 17 to 22 when the community perspective was added. However, there are some additional measures besides those displayed on the face of the steering wheel. The idea is to keep the display as simple as possible by showing those measures, which will have the most impact, but there are some secondary measures that are regularly tracked.

Reviewing results

The steering wheel is displayed prominently throughout the company. Each store has its own one-and-a-half metre square board that uses traffic light colours to highlight measures of success, need for improvement or concern. Blue is used for exceptional performance. Although there has been no detailed statistical analysis, those who work closely with the steering wheel are often able to predict what will happen in the next quarter based on the current results. If 'people' measures are showing a down turn, then this will need attention as it will have an impact on other segments in the next few quarters.

The results are communicated quarterly and management reviews also occur with that frequency, but there are weekly review meetings. Staff 'buy in' is important and there are town meetings and local reviews where objectives and targets are discussed.

Factors for success

The steering wheel works in Tesco because it is absolutely central to the way they run their business. It is the tool they use to roll out their strategy, manage performance and reward their people. Their CEO Sir Terry Leahy talks about it, and so do the staff in each of their stores. But to summarise some of the key attributes of the steering wheel, it is:

- Simple.
- Communicated extensively and regularly.
- Cascaded from top to bottom of the organisation.

- Based on metrics relevant to those being measured.
- Displayed in colour in prominent position.
- Linked to appraisal and reward.
- Reviewed frequently and regularly discussed.

As one executive put it:

'We tend to deliver what we are measured on – so it is important to have the right measures.'

A final word

Balanced Scorecards do work for many companies, but how you design, implement, use and update the scorecard really matters. In this book, we have tried to explain how we think this should be done, by presenting a set of tools, frameworks and experiences to help you. However, Balanced Scorecards require time and effort to get right, commitment to implement and perseverance to ensure they are used and updated. If you do not believe in the concept of performance measurement and using measures to help manage your business, then the Balanced Scorecard is not for you.

If you are going to implement or update a Balanced Scorecard in your organisation, are you prepared to put in the time and effort required?

If you are not, then we suggest that you do not start, as there are already too many companies with scorecards that are a shadow of what they should be because someone wanted to do it quickly.

If you are, then good luck. It will be a learning experience and should deliver great benefits to your organisation.

INSTANT TIP

Put the Balanced Scorecard at the centre of your management system.

References

Al-Najjar, M. and Neely, A. (1998) 'Customer Satisfaction Drivers and the Link to Financial Performance: Case Study', *Performance Measurement – Theory and Practice Conference,* Cambridge.

Bourne, M. C. S., Mills, J. F., Wilcox, M., Neely, A. D. and Platts, K, W. (2000) 'Designing, implementing and updating performance measurement systems', *International Journal of Production and Operations Management* 20(7): 754-71.

Buchanan, D. and Huczynski, A. (1997) *Organizational Behaviour,* 3rd edn, London: Prentice Hall.

Buckingham, M. and Coffman, C. (1999) *First Break All the Rules: What the World's Greatest Managers Do Differently,* London: Simon & Schuster.

Eccles, R. G. and Pyburn, P. J. (1992) 'Creating a Comprehensive System to Measure Performance', *Management Accounting* [US], October, pp. 41–44.

Franco, M. and Bourne, M. C. S. (2004) 'Are strategic performance measurement systems really effective?', *Proceedings of the 11th EurOMA annual conference*, Fontainebleau, 27-29 June.

Kaplan, R. S. and Norton, D. P. (1992) 'The balanced scorecard – measures that drive performance', *Harvard Business Review*, January/February, pp. 71–79.

Kaplan, R. S. and Norton, D. P. (1996) *The balanced scorecard – translating strategy into action*, Boston, MA: Harvard Business School Press.

Lewin, K. (1951) *Field Theory in Social Science*, New York, NY: Harper.

Lingle, J. H. and Schiemann, W. A. (1996) 'From Balanced Scorecard to Strategy Gauge: Is Measurement Worth It?', *Management Review,* March: 56–62.

Martinez, V., Kennerley, M., Wakelen, R., Hart, K. and Webb, J., (2006), *Impact of Performance Measurement and Management Systems*, Cranfield University School of Management Report.

Neely, A. D., Adams, C. and Kennerley, M. (2002) *The Performance Prism: The Scorecard for Measuring and Managing Business Success*, London: FT Prentice Hall.

Neely, A. D., Bourne, M. C. S., Mills, J. F., Richards, A. H. and Platts, K. W., (2002) *Strategy and performance: getting the measure of your business,* Cambridge: Cambridge University Press.

Neely, A. D., Mills, J. F., Gregory, M. J., Richards, A. H., Platts, K. W. and Bourne, M.C.S. (1996) *Getting the measure of your business*, London: Findlay.

Platts, K. W. (1994) 'Characteristics of methodologies for manufacturing strategy formulation', *Computer Integrated Manufacturing Systems*, 7(2): 93–99.

Rucci, A. J., Kirn, S. P. and Quinn, R. T. (1998) 'The employee-customer profit chain at Sears', *Harvard Business Review*, January/Febuary: 82–97.

Strebel, P. (1998) *The change pact: building commitment to ongoing change*, London: Financial Times Management.

http://www.sternstewart.com.
http://www.tomorrowscompany.com.

Index